Histories & Discourses

Histories & Discourses
Rewriting Constructivism

Siegfried J. Schmidt

Translated from the German by
Wolfram Karl Köck & Alison Rosemary Köck

imprint-academic.com

Copyright © Siegfried J. Schmidt, 2007

The moral rights of the author have been asserted.
No part of this publication may be reproduced in any form
without permission, except for the quotation of brief passages
in criticism and discussion.

Published in the UK by
Imprint Academic, PO Box 200, Exeter EX5 5YX, UK

Published in the USA by
Imprint Academic, Philosophy Documentation Center
PO Box 7147, Charlottesville, VA 22906-7147, USA

ISBN-13: 978184540 096 5

A CIP catalogue record for this book is available from the
British Library and US Library of Congress

Original publication:
Siegfried J. Schmidt, *Geschichten & Diskurse. Abschied vom
Konstruktivismus*. Mit einem Vorwort von Mike Sandbothe.
Reinbek bei Hamburg: Rowohlt Verlag GmbH. 2003.

Contents

	Introduction by Mike Sandbothe	1
	Preface	19
1	The Basic Mechanism —Supposition and Presupposition	23
2	Models of Reality	31
3	Culture Programmes	35
4	Interim Summary 1	45
5	Histories and Discourses	49
6	Agency	63
7	Communication	71
8	Process-dependent Realities	87
9	Beyond Dualism	99
10	Interim Summary 2	105
11	Identity	115
12	Morality	127
13	Truth	143
14	Interim Summary 3	159
15	Why a Theory of Histories&Discourses?	161
	Glossaries	173
	Selected References	177

Introduction

by Mike Sandbothe

The name of Siegfried J. Schmidt is closely associated in Germany with the cross-disciplinary research programme of Radical Constructivism (Schmidt 1987, 1991 et al.). The author has, in the meantime, distanced himself from the epithet of the Radical in a number of publications. Thus, in his widely read book, *Kognitive Autonomie und soziale Orientierung* (1994), moderate forms of culturalist discourse groundwork replace the naturalist foundation attempts previously designated as radical. But what is happening in Histories & Discourses (H&D)? Is the renowned co-founder, enthusiastic defender and successful promoter of constructivist thinking with his new book really (as stated in the preface) 'parting company with constructivism' and thus giving up his own research programme? Or does the rhetoric of the preface much rather indicate an internal movement of transformation, which aims to preserve key questions central to constructivist discourse and subject them to fresh scrutiny?

As an established paradigm of epistemological research, constructivism investigates the internal constitution of human epistemic capacities. This is traditionally a genuine philosophical enterprise. Philosophy, in contradistinction to other scientific fields, occupies itself with the thinking of thinking. Its object, for this reason, has a structure that is different from that of the objects of 'normal' fields of enquiry. The modern philosopher is not primarily concerned with researching a particular domain of objects (in economics, law, life, nature, culture etc.), but with the manner in which we distinguish objects as objects and epistemic spheres as epistemic spheres from each other, and thus constitute them as such, in the first place. The epistemological research programme of constructivism is part of this tradition of thought.

The strongest competitor of constructivist epistemologies is so-called realism. Constructivism is, therefore, frequently referred to as anti-realism. The realist's position is that the central accomplishment of human knowing consists in representing an independently existing reality as appropriately as possible. In contrast, the anti-realist, or constructivist, insists that we cannot possibly gain any neutral access to a reality that pre-exists our knowing—because we would have to know it already in order to be able to speak about it! —and that it is, therefore, more plausible to understand reality not as a presupposition but as a product of human knowing.

Constructivism in its radical form believed it could prove the correctness of its professed anti-realist epistemology by recourse to scientific research results from biology, neurophysiology and cognitive psychology (Schmidt 1982a/b). From this perspective, the brain is seen as an autonomous constructor of realities, whose operations constantly refer to its very own operations, because it can perceive all external stimuli only as irritations and is forced to process them in its own unique neuronal language. The untenability of naturalist strategies of argument lies in the fact that the recourse to the allegedly objective evidential value of neurobiological research results ignores that any consistent application of constructivist theory must reveal these results to be constructions as well and, consequently, to possess no value as evidence to convince the realists (Janich 1992).

Reacting to arguments of this kind, Schmidt attempted, in *Kognitive Autonomie und soziale Orientierung* (1994), to replace the naturalist rationales he had previously promoted himself with culturalist ones. The point of departure of his argument was the idea that human observers do not carry out their operations in an 'unmarked space' as had been implied by the constructivist logic of distinction from Spencer Brown to Niklas Luhmann. Schmidt, therefore, adopting Kenneth J. Gergen's Social Constructionism, postulated that human observers 'at all times' operate in a space that is deeply 'marked' culturally and socio-structurally (Schmidt 1994, 47). The central objective of the 1994 book was to develop a constructivist version of the hermeneutical thesis of irreducibility and to render it plausible by recourse to empirical research results from the cultural and social sciences.

In H&D, at variance with *Kognitive Autonomie und soziale Orientierung,* Schmidt not only changes the scientific domain of reference chosen to support his foundational strategy, but this very strategy itself. The endeavour to render constructivist thinking plausible in an empirical way by combinatorially exploiting selected research results from various scientific disciplines is given up in favour of the decidedly philosophical form of argument of discursive self-grounding. Its aim is the explication of that which we always inevitably have to presuppose in all our thinking, speaking and acting, namely, sense.

Scholars investigating cultures and media do not normally care to examine the sense of 'sense'. Instead, they consider sense as given and concern themselves with the ways in which it is communicated culturally through the media. Schmidt proceeds in just the same way in the two books devoted exclusively to problems of media and communication study, which he published after his move from literary studies at Siegen University to communication studies at the University of Münster (Schmidt 2000; Schmidt/Zurstiege 2000). In H&D, however, Schmidt is not writing as an expert in media and communication studies but as a philosopher of culture and language. And this for very good reasons. They have to do with Schmidt's conception of media and communication study.

Schmidt's underpinning of this conception in cultural studies was presented in *Kalte Faszination* (2000), and spelt out subsequently in terms of his specialist discipline, together with Guido Zurstiege, in *Orientierung Kommunikationswissenschaft* (2000). Of particular importance here is the 'integrative media concept' (Schmidt 2000, 93), developed under the heading 'compact concept "medium" ' (2000, 94). Regarding this concept, the author writes in H&D: 'As explained in various places, I conceive of language not as a medium but as an instrument of communication. Media — beginning with writing — I understand as a compact concept systemically integrating four component-domains: communication instruments such as language and images; sets of technical implements (from pen and paper to internet technology); the social-systemic organisation of the exploitation of these implements (e.g. scriptoria, publishing or broadcasting houses); the media offers resulting from the combined action of these components.'

From this definition we can indirectly infer that instruments of communication differ from media by the fact that they can function without sets of technical implements, without social institutions, and without the media offerings produced and/or distributed with their help. At first sight, this appears convincing. Whenever we are speaking to each other face to face, we do not, in normal circumstances, need any technical speaking aids, nor do we have to rely on media institutions to make sure that our messages reach their addressees. This is precisely what distinguishes natural face-to-face communication from technically mediated distance-communication. At the same time, however, Schmidt insists that technically and socially implemented media systems cannot function without the sense products that we generate with the help of communication instruments such as language and images. Even though these may not themselves be media, they are nevertheless indispensable components of media for the simple reason that they supply the sense resources that are stored, processed and distributed by media.

Against this backdrop it becomes understandable why Schmidt, with H&D, carries out a change of perspective from media and communication studies to studies of culture and the philosophy of language. Answering the question of the conditions of the possibility of sense requires the focused thematisation of those communication instruments that, although presupposed by media and communication studies as components of the media concept, are still not being properly investigated as such. Accordingly, one may indeed state, in Schmidt's preferred terminology, that the subject of philosophy of culture and language is the 'blind spot' which is constitutive of media and communication studies, and which therefore eludes them.

The very title of Schmidt's book makes it plain that he is out to explore the sense-generating mechanism of human communication instruments from the perspective of a 'histories&discourses-philosophy'. This novel theory proposal is developed in detail for the first time in the present book. In order to appreciate its significance, one must be prepared to share a considerable number of basic assumptions. Histories and discourses are the result of the operation of a conceptual mechanism of distinction that allegedly underlies all natural languages as the condition of the possibility of sense. Schmidt describes this 'basic mechanism' as the 'auto-constitutive interdependency of supposition (…) and presupposition (…)'. What is this supposed to mean?

Whenever we perform an action, think a thought, or experience an emotion, we make a selection (usually unconsciously) from a spectrum of possible actions, thoughts or emotions, and choose (again frequently unconsciously) the action, the thought, or the emotion that we choose. By deciding in this way, we move something into the centre of our attention, and not something else (X instead of Y). We enact a supposition that is itself only possible under the condition that other suppositions have previously taken place. These prior suppositions Schmidt calls presuppositions. They become apparent only whenever I enact a concrete supposition, i.e. they are themselves, *qua* presuppositions of a particular supposition, dependent on this supposition. For this reason, Schmidt speaks of an auto-constitutive interdependency between supposition and presupposition. The presupposition is the condition of the supposition and the supposition is the condition of the presupposition. The one engenders the other; the interdependency of supposition and presupposition generates itself, i.e. is auto-constitutive.

The function of those sense structures which Schmidt calls 'histories&discourses' is to facilitate the selection of a prospective supposition from a set of possible suppositions. Histories and discourses function like 'directories of selection for pending selections'. They relieve individual agents 'of the neuroticising relentless reflection on why they do A and not B to Z, and why they talk about Alpha and not about Beta to Omega'. This means in practice: the histories that I have experienced and heard in my life, and that I can recall for myself and others by means of narrations, will help me in concrete action situations to choose a particular action by way of distinction from other possible actions. The situation is similar for those discourses in which I participate myself. They throw into relief particular speech acts against others, particular expressions of emotions against others, and they help me in concrete communication situations to decide for a particular speech act or a particular expression of emotion.

As complex frameworks of interactive dependencies, histories and discourses are closely entwined. For discourses are, *qua* performances, themselves actions and consequently embedded in histories, and histories are, *qua* meaningfulness, themselves communications and consequently embedded in discourses. The distinction between histories (specified as interdependent actions) and discourses (specified as interdependent communications) is, therefore, introduced by the author as a contingent but functional category of observation. Correspondingly, Schmidt in no way postulates histories&discourses 'as the prime foundations on which to erect a theory systematically', despite their central importance in his theoretical edifice. Much rather, the histories in which I am enmeshed and the discourses in which I participate, are themselves suppositions resting on presuppositions. Schmidt describes these presuppositions as the interplay between models of reality and culture programmes, which precedes histories and discourses.

Models of reality consist of the total spectrum of categories and semantic differentiations that is available to a society as its 'system of options with regard to (...) sense orientation'. Among the categories are 'e.g. age, sex, power, possessions, kinship, food, or clothing'. The semantic differentiations (old/young, male/female etc.) operationalise the categories, prepare them for use in concrete communication processes. The task of culture programmes is to establish effective 'difference management' in the handling of the given model of reality. For this purpose, particular categories and semantic differentiations are interwoven according to life-practical criteria, are culturally marked out against others and socially habitualised.

The complex apparatus of concepts developed by Schmidt in his book, and systematically assembled in the form of glossaries in an appendix, is intended by the author to meet 'the central claims of constructivist thought'. These claims consist in securing 'the full justification of the theory by itself and its consistent application to itself'. In the understanding of the author, his 'parting company with constructivism' is, therefore, no parting company with the 'claims of constructivist thought'. It is instead to be understood as a critique of naturalist and/or culturalist forms of argumentation, which had become associated with the notion of constructivism. Their place is now to be taken by an alternative, self-grounding constructivism.

The chief difference to the 'socio-cultural constructivism' (Schmidt 1994, 47) of 1994 may be elucidated by means of the new problem-solving strategy proposed by the author in H&D for the 'mediation between cognitive autonomy and social orientation'. 'Cognitive autonomy' refers to the fact that the suppositions I make must always be classified strictly as 'my very own' suppositions, because 'agents' (i.e. human beings) — according to the fundamental presupposition of constructivism that is still upheld by Schmidt — 'can only operate in a strictly system-specific manner'. Everything I say, do or feel, I may indeed say, do, or feel in accordance with suppositions and presuppositions, which I have acquired through socialising cultural training, and which may, on the basis of models of reality and culture programmes, concretise themselves in histories and discourses. The cognitive realisation of an action, a thought or an emotion is, however, a cognitive realisation in my own head and, therefore, strictly individual and not accessible to, or re-enactable by, anyone except myself.

This fundamental problem of constructivism remains a problem also of the self-grounding theory proposal. Under the conditions of the 'histories&discourses-philosophy', however, it appears to be a problem whose novel description seems, at the same time, to imply its resolution. The validity of the intersubjective reference to reality by my actions, thoughts and emotions, is sufficiently secured already by the generative 'mechanism of reflexivity' that is, after all, responsible for the functioning of the complex network of suppositions/presuppositions, model of reality/culture programme, and histories/discourses. The 'concept of structural coupling' that had served to connect directly the cognitions operating in exclusively system-specific ways, has thereby been made expendable. This signifies one of the fundamental differences that separate the 'post-constructivist' constructivism of H&D both from the naturalist and the culturalist strategies of argument as practised by previous constructivisms.

The heart of the matter in Schmidt's new book is, therefore, the anatomy of the reflection-theoretical conditions of the possibility, which support the socio-cultural network of 'parameters of control', with whose help individual praxis may, at all events, transform itself into social praxis. The author even goes so far as to derive the spatio-temporally situated consciousness, the agents and their socialisation, and also the 'complementary relationship between consciousness and object' from the 'logic of supposition and presupposition'. This logic, designed as an auto-constitutive process of reciprocal generation, indicates the 'non-dualist' strategy of foundation underlying Schmidt's theoretical edifice.

The strategy consists in dissolving the 'problems of dualistic philosophical thinking by the deliberate shifting of the starting manoeuvre from objects to processes'. The old oppositions of subject and object, statement and object, schema and content, are thus processualised and, in the Hegelian sense of the word, 'sublated' onto a higher-level form of thought. On a meta-theoretical plane, consequently, the requirement results to redefine the basic constructivist goal past the opposition of realism/anti-realism. In this respect, the histories&discourses-philosophy quite justifiably presents itself as 'parting company with constructivism'. For the essential sustaining sense of self of constructivism has so far been nourished to a considerable extent by its opposition to realism.

Schmidt's joining the ranks of the promoters of 'non-dualist philosophical approaches' brings to mind not only the explicitly named Josef Mitterer and Peter Janich but primarily the pragmatist currents of modern philosophical thinking which are, at present, enjoying an international renaissance (Sandbothe 2000 and 2003a). Thus Richard Rorty—one of the principal representatives of American neo-pragmatism—presents his position in the tradition of John Dewey and Donald Davidson as decidedly anti-dualist. In contradistinction to Schmidt, however, Rorty advocates a kind of thinking that no longer deals with epistemological questions constructively and systematically, but solely destructively and therapeutically. Rorty does not, therefore, develop a complex procedure to processualise self and world but simply and curtly proposes to thrust aside quite rigorously all epistemological problems of any kind. The epistemological textbook questions about the 'conditions of the possibility of X' should, in his opinion, be replaced with quite different thematic fields (i.e. fields of immediate socio-political relevance)(Rorty 1999).

Not so Schmidt. In his view, the one—i.e. the democratic orientation of a pragmatistically envisaged science—can and must not exclude or even replace the other—i.e. the (reflection-theoretically processualised) epistemology. The internal intertwining of both domains is shown in chapters 11-14 of the present book, which deal with personal and social identity, morality and truth. There Schmidt demonstrates how the interplay of suppositions and presuppositions, models of reality and culture programmes, histories and discourses, realises itself as a societal process under the reflexive conditions of the mutual observation of agents.

In order to attain an adequate understanding of Schmidt's proposal, according to which identity, morality and truth must be described as 'orientation-orientations', one must first of all realise clearly that a non-dualist philosophy *sensu* Schmidt is not at all concerned with the reality status, of whatever kind, of suppositions and presuppositions, models of reality and culture programmes, histories and discourses. Instead, these sense-generating structures are melted down to 'operative fictions' that acquire their pragmatic efficiency through the reciprocal ascriptions by means of which agents impute to other agents moral rules of action, verifiable sets of knowledge, and affectively charged identities.

This is a clever move. A baroque system of symbolic orders of the first, second or third plane of being is thus replaced by intersubjective ascription practices amenable to observation along varying lines. As for morality, this leads to devising it as 'the histories&discourses-bound application of moral orientation principles'. Moral principles are not regarded as 'norms of a universal kind', which would require an ethical (i.e. theoretical) justification, but as auto-constitutive ascription practices that prove their mettle through their action-guiding function in a particular culture *qua* 'pragmatic legitimation interrupters'.

Schmidt proceeds similarly with regard to 'truth'. Truth is specified as the unity of the difference true/false and serves to secure 'statement reliability in histories and discourses'. This is achieved, on the one hand, by the approving application of 'true/false' as 'the interrupter of arguments by virtue of the legitimacy of the reference to the *status quo* of shared knowledge'; and, on the other hand, by the forewarning application of 'true/false', which safeguards that 'a renewed corroboration of truth can be demanded any time'. Both modes of application were elaborated in 20th century pragmatist philosophy and brought into play as alternatives to classical conceptions of truth, which attempt to explain the potential consensuality of a statement by recourse to its truth *qua* correspondence (Davidson/Rorty 2004 and Sandbothe 2003b).

With regard to morality and truth, Schmidt argues as an uncompromising pragmatist. The case is more complex with identity. It functions as the structural presupposition for the ascription of the two orienting differences of true/false and good/evil, whose reflexive dynamics Schmidt also describes as knowledge-related 'expectation-expectation' and value-related 'imputation-imputation'. Now, identity is certainly ascribed, and thus an operative fiction. In contradistinction to truth and morality, however, personal (ego/alter) and social identity (we/the others) are, in Schmidt's view, not just networks of ascriptions but, moreover, conditions of the possibility of all ascription.

According to Schmidt, this is necessarily so because the identical self is 'the point of departure for all references of consciousness and the domain of reference for the self-ascription of intentions, action capability, will etc.'. Schmidt describes the relationship between ego and alter as a process of reciprocal self-supposition so as to be able to derive formal self-identity (in analogy to consciousness and its objects) through the logic of supposition and presupposition. It is only the close examination of its 'specificity' that then relates the formation of identity, in a second step, to the 'selectivity of histories and the participation of agents in discourses as well as (…) agents' imagination and creativity'. And herein lies the difference to the identity concept of pragmatism, according to which 'a person is nothing but a coherent and plausible set of beliefs and desires' (Rorty 1988, 44).

The proximity of Schmidt's histories&discourses-philosophy to pragmatist intentions and ideas has thus become evident. At the same time, however, it must be pointed out that this proximity has to do with questions concerning details of its execution and not with the design of the total enterprise. The difference in design is reflected in the detail of the difference between Schmidt's concept of identity and the pragmatist model of the person. Whereas Schmidt sets up truth and morality in connection with the allegedly antecedent conditions of histories and discourses, he specifies identity firstly and primarily as the formal condition of the possibility of histories and discourses, and only secondarily and in terms of content as their realisation. This makes clear that Schmidt's argument follows a foundational dimension that is directed at histories and discourses but, at the same time, also transcends them. We have here the already introduced 'auto-constitutive interdependency of supposition (…) and presupposition (…)'.

The logic of this interdependency, which Schmidt traces back to Hegel, is intended to safeguard 'the full justification of the theory by itself and its consistent application to itself'. The theory conception implied by this approach is diametrically opposed to the theory conception promoted by pragmatism. The pragmatist proposes to replace the theoretical claim to self-grounding and self-explanation, which has been driving philosophical thinking for ages, with a socio-political criterion of utility. In the final chapter of his book Schmidt does, in fact, raise the pragmatist question 'Why a theory of histories&ddiscourses?'. However, in contradistinction to Rorty's pragmatism, Schmidt does not simply presuppose the manifold criteria of utility resulting from the socio-political value standards of modern democracies, as a contingent frame of values. Instead he puts forward the claim to prepare, with his histories&discourses-philosophy, the epistemological foundation for 'the essential decision in favour of democratic forms of social life'.

It is no accident that Schmidt raises problems of 'multiculturalism and globalisation' in this context. For precisely in their external relationships, democratic societies will, under the conditions of their globalisation, require good arguments to convince the members of non-democratic societies of the advantages of their democratisation. Whether the theoretical recourse to the auto-constitutive interdependency of suppositions&presuppositions, reality-models&culture-programmes, and histories&discourses will actually set free the necessary trans-cultural power of conviction, is for the future to prove. One must not forget, however, that Schmidt's book is clearly intended for an intellectual public that is well-versed in cultural studies and well-adapted to constructivist thinking. His considerations of criteria of utility relate to the effects that the histories&discourses-philosophy may have on selected disseminators (and through their mediation on decision-makers in global economy and politics).

Taking into account this realistic assessment of the potential impact of the present work, Schmidt's approach can be interpreted as opening up future prospects even, and especially, from a pragmatist perspective. For most of the contemporary scholars in cultural studies, who were during their academic training styled by schools of thought critical of both enlightenment and democracy — and no small number! —, might perhaps be more amenable to rigorous reflection-theoretical figures of argument, and might, consequently, in their work once again lend greater weight to the basic democratic endeavour and the associated sociopolitical questions. Thus one can only hope that the histories&discourses-philosophy is accorded an equally engaging reception in the first decade of the 21st century as was granted to Radical Constructivism in the last decade of the past millennium.

References cited

Davidson, Donald/Rorty, Richard (2004): Wozu Wahrheit? Eine Debatte, ed. von Mike Sandbothe, Frankfurt.: Suhrkamp.
Janich, Peter (1992): 'Die methodische Ordnung von Konstruktionen. Der Radikale Konstruktivismus aus der Sicht des Erlanger Konstruktivismus', in: Schmidt (ed.), 1991, 14-41.
Rorty, Richard (1988): *Solidarität oder Objektivität?*, Stuttgart: Reclam.
Rorty, Richard (1999): *Philosophy and Social Hope*, London und New York: Penguin.
Sandbothe, Mike (2000) (ed.): *Die Renaissance des Pragmatismus. Aktuelle Verflechtungen zwischen analytischer und kontinentaler Philosophie*, Weilerswist: Velbrück Wissenschaft.
Sandbothe, Mike (2003a): 'Medien – Kommunikation – Kultur. Grundlagen einer pragmatischen Kulturwissenschaft', in: *Kulturwissenschaft als Kommunikationswissenschaft*: Projekte, Probleme, Perspektiven, hg. von Matthias Karmasin und Carsten Winter, Opladen: Westdeutscher Verlag, 257-271.
Sandbothe, Mike (2003b): 'Davidson and Rorty on Truth: Reshaping Analytic Philosophy for a Transcontinental Conversation', in: *A House Divided: Comparing Analytic and Continental Philosophers*, hg. von Carlos G. Prado, Amherst (NY): Humanity Books, 135-258.
Schmidt, Siegfried J. (1982a): 'Unsere Welt – und das ist alles', in: *Merkur. Deutsche Zeitschrift für europäisches Denken*, Heft 4, Jahrgang 36, April, 356-366.
Schmidt, Siegfried J. (1982b): 'Einladung, Maturana zu lesen', in: Humberto R. Maturana, *Erkennen: die Organisation und Verkörperung von Wirklichkeit*, Braunschweig and Wiesbaden: Vieweg 1982, 1-10.
Schmidt, Siegfried J. (1987) (ed.): *Der Diskurs des Radikalen Konstruktivismus*, Frankfurt/M.: Suhrkamp.
Schmidt, Siegfried J. (1991) (ed.): *Kognition und Gesellschaft. Der Diskurs des Radikalen Konstruktivismus 2*, Frankfurt/M.: Suhrkamp.
Schmidt, Siegfried J. (1994): *Kognitive Autonomie und soziale Orientierung. Konstruktivistische Bemerkungen zum Zusammenhang von Kognition, Kommunikation, Medien und Kultur*, Frankfurt/M.: Suhrkamp.
Schmidt, Siegfried J. (2000): *Kalte Faszination. Medien Kultur Wissenschaft in der Mediengesellschaft*, Weilerswist: Velbrück Wissenschaft.

Schmidt, Siegfried J. (2003): *Geschichten und Diskurse. Abschied vom Konstruktivismus*, Reinbek bei Hamburg: Rowohlt.
Schmidt, Siegfried J. / Zurstiege, Guido (2000): Orientierung Kommunikationswissenschaft. Was sie kann, was sie will, Reinbek bei Hamburg: Rowohlt.

Preface

Constructivism is beginning to show its years, G. Schiepeck noted recently, and so we may, and really should, ask ourselves how it has been managing and what has become of it. G. Roth claims that constructivism is meanwhile so widely accepted in scientific discourse that its basic tenets can be taken for granted. Others, however, believe, e.g. N. Groeben, that it has at long last been totally discredited by the counter-arguments put forward (not least by himself), and has finally been exposed as nothing but a theoretical aberration and baseless exaggeration.

In my 1994 book, *Cognitive Autonomy and Social Orientation*, I proposed that the constructivism of the day, whose foundations were primarily biological and psychological, should be given an (additional) socio-cultural underpinning and also include an appropriate account of emotions, in order to encompass adequately not only biological and psychological but also microsociological and macrosociological aspects.

This proposal was, on the whole, well received. However, critics (especially J. Mitterer and St. Weber) still contended that this variant of constructivist theory adaptation remained trapped in a *dualist* theory format, if only because of its distinction between actuality and reality.

In the present study,[1] I part company with some of the sets of problems central to the discourse of Radical Constructivism, in particular the question of the reality of reality, the relationship between actuality and reality, and the construction of 'construction'. This departure does not consist in a way of resolving the problems in question but instead adopts the form of their dissolution in a new theory of histories&discourses. This theory parts company with some of the variants of the discourse of constructivism, in particular those lines of argument which are (still) conditioned by close ties with biology and cognitive science and which surreptitiously maintain that these sciences guarantee their accuracy and significance. For precisely this reason, however, one of the central claims of constructivist thought is defeated, namely the full justification of the theory by itself and its consistent application to itself. I finally part company with all those variants of 'vulgar constructivism' which only keep churning out mantra-like that everything is constructed without offering any plausible exposition of the involved notion of construction.

The general aim of the present study is to overcome the dualism of traditional constructivist discourse by avoiding any ontological imputation and by construing all the relevant thematic object domains in question exclusively as process results. Thus, the often-used constructivist formula that the construction of reality can be conceived of as the reality of construction, is made plausible step by step. And my concern is not just the construction of objects in an everyday sense, but also the construction of consciousness, space and time, agency and identity, action and communi-

---

[1] This study owes to Sebastian Jünger's thesis (Kultur, Kognition, Kommunikation—Aspekte integrativer Theoriearbeit. Wiesbaden: DUV 2002) more than the quotations reveal, i.e. primarily the challenge to bring (once more) order (of a kind) into my thoughts.

cation, morality and truth, through the self-grounding processes of supposition and presupposition and the generative mechanism of reflexivity.

Central to my considerations are two problems which I consider to be fundamental problems of human action:

- Whatever we do, we always (consciously or unconsciously) select a possibility from the set of possibilities that we can envisage concretely but do not realise in the given situation. Selection necessarily constitutes contingency, and vice versa. Coping with contingency is, therefore, a permanent task of human social life.

- The selections we make are the selections *we* make. In making them we remain bound by the specific conditions of selection given for us. This agent-specific situation, in the constructivist discourse known as 'cognitive autonomy', must however be reconciled with the conditions of the social orientation of agents, in order to enable them to act and communicate in a socially adequate way. The second fundamental problem of human life is, therefore, the mediation between cognitive autonomy and social orientation.

The solutions I am going to offer for these problems in the following will be oriented, in the first place, by what the mechanism of *reflexivity* can accomplish. This accomplishment consists primarily in managing (universal) contingency by means of (specific) contingency, thereby reducing the risks of contingency, i.e. the insecurity and instability of our actions, by such socially relevant orientation-orientations (termed 'operative fictions') in thought, action and communication, as are compatible with the agents' cognitive autonomy. In other words, the principle of the solution is not to control contingency through a maximally objective harmonisation with reality, but to withdraw it from the observation of all agents by means of the fictitious reference to their mutually attributed collective knowledge, i.e. by 'rendering it invisible'.

In a nutshell, the course of the following reflections could be summed up by the formula: from the start without a beginning through the building of structures out of instabilities to the finality of transience.

In writing down these reflections, I would very much have liked to follow Elfriede Gerstl's recommendation: 'everything one can say one can also say in passing' — but I am afraid that I have been only partially successful.

PS. The first version of this text was composed in the serenity of the great Namib Desert. I dedicate this book to all those at the Desert Lodge Rostock Ritz whose loving care made my labour a delight.

My gratitude also extends to all the employees of the Internationales Forschungszentrum Kulturwissenschaften in Vienna where I was able to create the final version of this book during a sabbatical term in the winter 2002/2003.

1
The Basic Mechanism – Supposition and Presupposition

Whatever we do, we do it in the gestalt of a supposition: we do something, and not something else, although we could have done so; and such a supposition always takes a certain gestalt for us and — should we be under observation — also for others: it is a supposition of type A and not type B, C, M or X.

As far as we can judge within a lifetime, every single supposition that we are making here and now has been preceded by other suppositions to which we (can) relate more or less consciously. All our suppositions to date therefore form a context of suppositions in given concrete situations. We can now refer to this context by way of memories and narratives. This context of suppositions comprises the totality of our prior life experiences that will, in turn, in every concrete situation affect our future experiences as expectations.

Every supposition makes at least one presupposition. As a rule, however, many presuppositions are made or drawn upon — consider, for instance, how many presuppositions must be fulfilled before we can begin to open a car door or ski down a slope. The nexus between supposition and pre-supposition is auto-constitutive as neither can be meaningfully envisaged without the other. Supposition and presupposition are, therefore, strictly *complementary*. The presupposition of a supposition can only be observed in the reflexive reference to the supposition (cf. S. Jünger 2002: 47). If one accepts the auto-constitution of supposition and presupposition, then one also accepts that there can be no presupposition-free beginning—the only possible beginning is to make a supposition.

G. W. F. Hegel, the originator of the concepts of supposition [*Setzung*, lit.= positing] and pre-supposition [*Voraus-Setzung*], in his *Wissenschaft der Logik* specified the act of knowing as '... an act of supposing [= positing] that immediately determines itself equally as an act of pre-supposing', and he thus evidently described a self-constituting process (or perhaps one should rather say: a mechanism?) that underlies not only all knowing but also all action. In the following I shall try to elaborate this fundamental idea step by step.

Whether we perceive or describe something, ponder something or become consciously aware of something as something particular, we are always executing a serious game of distinctions. We (and not anyone else) describe (and not explain) something as that particular something (and not as something else). In doing so we make use of linguistic resources whose semantic potential and social acceptance is tacitly presumed and, at the same time, by this very use confirmed as 'viable' (i.e. as manageable or successful in the understanding of E. von Glasersfeld). All this is realised (meaning nothing but: all this we can envisage or think in this way only, not in any other) as a happening in a particular situation at a particular point in time, i.e. in a context of suppositions.

Suppositions constitute contingency because they must be selective with reference to other options. As selections they are decisions, and only *qua* decisions do they make contingency *observable*. This means that selection and contingency must be envisaged jointly, they constitute each other, they are strictly complementary.

If the operation of distinction is of such universal and weighty significance, the question poses itself what conditions it requires.

In order to distinguish A from B, A and B must be distinguishable from something else, say C. As S. Jünger has shown, observing must therefore be construed as a *twofold* process of differentiation, '… that allows the differentiation between A and B only on the basis of the differentiation of A *and* B, i.e. that emerges as the differentiation between C and [A and B] in an observation of the second order. And it is not at all simplistic but necessary to base this first-order observation on a second-order observation that must, of course, itself be set up, through a new observation, as a relation between D and {C and [A and B]}. Observing is, therefore, a dynamic three-part relation that must, however, assert itself as a two-part relation because it can only be identified as a three-part relation by further observation.' (2002:30 f.)

Every supposition, according to the logic of the present argument, requires a positing instance that is affirmed by the very act of supposition. In the case of cognitive suppositions (e.g. perceptions), we call the positing instance *consciousness*. Consciousness operates on all levels by means of *reference* through the auto-constitutive interdependency of supposition (consciousness *of* something) and presupposition (without consciousness *no* something). The presupposition of a supposition can only be observed (posited) as such by way of reflexive reference and thus repeats the game of supposition and presupposition. It is only by virtue of reflexivity that references can be recognised and communicated. Consciousness is the irreducible condition for dealing with consciousness, and reflexivity is the condition for becoming aware of consciousness. S. Jünger has devised the following conceptualisation of the problem of consciousness: 'thinking about' presupposes 'something' as an identifiable unit of differentiation, this distinction being simultaneously an act of positing. Where there is thinking, the interruption of continuous processes creates structures. These interruptions make the particular dynamics reflexive and thus allow for the emergence of order.

Reference or *relationality* as the principle of consciousness, *reflexivity* allowing reference to presuppositions, the community-forming imputations of such relations in others, and the *selective auto-constitution* of the context of supposition and presupposition, seem to be the elementary principles or 'mechanisms' driving all our actions and making them accessible to observation and interpretation. In the following I shall seek to explore where an application of these elementary mechanisms leads us in the development of our theories.

*

Consider an example. We observe something in our environment as young, thus unconsciously making use of the semantic distinction young/old. This distinction must necessarily be presupposed because otherwise we could not in our act of judgment decide between young and old. But what do we refer to when observing and judging? In our example it is age. It is obvious that the decision for one side of a difference (e.g. young) presupposes the unity of the difference young/old (i.e. age). If I do not possess the semantic category age, then I cannot differentiate it into all the possible shades of linguistic meaning between 'very young' and 'very old' and remain unable to perceive and differentially name something *as* old or *as* young. S. Jünger formulates, '... that observing *either* difference *or* unity becomes possible only by implicitly presupposing the respective other, i.e. that which is not actually under observation. Difference is only observable as a unity, and unity only in difference.' (2002:37) Differences, therefore, mark interconnectedness rather than exclusion. The operative use of one side of a difference keeps the unclaimed other side on hold, as it were. Without unobservables, Jünger says, no observables; observables and unobservables, discontinuity and continuity, are complementary (2002:50).

*

Three important observational points of view have emerged in my analysis so far, designated without further specification as *categories, semantic differentiations,* and *distinctions*.

- Categories, in the theoretical conception developed here, mark societally relevant *dimensions of meaning*, e.g. age, sex, power, possessions, kinship, food, or clothing. Categories may be described as nodes in a network of categories, which attain distinctness and semantic profile by virtue of their difference from other categories (age vs. appearance vs. health etc.). Without such a difference even categories 'cannot make sense', and so we must again conclude that there must be a unity of the difference between categories that organises the basically infinite diversity of categories in a network, thus permitting selective reference.

Furthermore, I consider it plausible to assume that this network has developed and proved its mettle in a society's history of problem-solving and environmental adaptation, and that it can therefore co-orient the actions of the members of the society because it remains practically unchallenged, although it can certainly be observed to change on a long-term basis. I call this network, i.e. the unity of the differences between categories, *model of reality*, to be understood as a model *for* realities (cf. chapter 2).

- The reference to categories is differentiated through action and communication and thus concretised into a smaller or larger number of semantic differentiations of the categories, e.g. binary or n-ary ones (dead/alive, but also freezing/cold/tepid/warm/hot). Semantic differentiations are *processes*, dynamic arrangements, which must continually be generated anew; they are not invariably fixed entities. They render categories describable by breaking down the unity of the differentiations or differences, i.e. the category, into distinguishable semantic suppositions. In the process of semantic differentiation, the semantic potential of categories is, as it were, operationalised for concrete processes of cognition and communication.

- Whenever a particular supposition is made, i.e. a (symmetrical) semantic differentiation is transformed into an (asymmetrical) distinction ('a pretty young girl' and not 'an ugly old man'), then — more or less consciously — *one* option is selected from the pool of available semantic differentiations, which gains its semantic valency by virtue of the difference from the other possibilities of semantic differentiation: young, pretty, and girl 'make sense' by exploiting the implicit but unobserved difference from old, ugly, and man, with reference to the categories age, appearance and sex. In this sense, supposition and presupposition are mutually auto-constitutive and confirm each other in every process of supposition: suppositions operate on the basis of presuppositions, presuppositions orient the meaning attribution of suppositions. Consequently, categories can be described as the unities of the difference between semantic differentiations and distinctions.

These reflections also make clear why categories and semantic differentiations can only meaningfully be devised as cross-temporal and agent-independent; solely on this condition can they socially co-orient agents as autonomous decision-making systems, because every agent is convinced that all the others rely on the same presuppositions in an identical or at least sufficiently comparable manner. We simply cannot envisage an alternative to this unconscious transference of individual cognitive developments onto others, and we are therefore fully justified in our belief that the world must appear pretty similar to all the others, and that they themselves also share this our conviction. This *mode of reflexivity of the collective expectation of collective expectation* (expectation of expectation) I shall from now on call *operative fiction*.

However, categories and semantic differentiations become effective in controlling actions only as soon as supposition-competent instances (henceforth called 'agents') actually apply these orientation options in concrete contexts of action and communication for purposes of reference, i.e. for distinctions and designations, thus enacting agent-related suppositions in temporally and spatially concrete situations and thereby exploiting these semantic presuppositions. The complementary interdependence between suppositions and presuppositions, therefore, calls for agents that activate this connection and keep it going.

Suppositions and presuppositions form an auto-constitutive nexus of mutual dependency that produces its specific 'reality' through the *effectiveness* of the references for agents, and not through an appeal to a specific ontological arrangement in 'the reality'.

Finally, the constitutive interconnection between suppositions and presuppositions also decides about constellations of observation. Observers of the first order (agents in their daily activities) enact suppositions without conscious reference to their presuppositions. Observers of the second order set in motion processes of observation in order to observe the presuppositions of the suppositions made by first-order observers, their own presuppositions functioning as blind spots. Observers of the third order observe the presuppositions of the observers of the second order with the help of their blind spots etc. This hierarchical arrangement in no way implies an ascending scale of increasing quality, but simply identifies *directions* of observation as they are practised in everyday life, in scientific research or in the philosophy of science.

2
Models of Reality

The system of options with regard to the sense orientation of a society, consisting of categories and semantic differentiations, was introduced in chapter 1 as the *model of reality* of a society. It is specified as the collective knowledge of the members of a society about 'their world', which has been generated by action and which has continually been systematised and corroborated by the experiences deriving from such action. Collective knowledge is not to be understood as an entity but as the process-result of reflexivity, thus encompassing the cognitive 'content' of the expectation-expectations that agents attribute to each other as collective knowledge in the sense of an operative fiction.

A model of reality is established by the social-reflexive references of agents enacted through actions and communications, and it is solidified as a symbolic-semantic order by language. Language permits the schematised designation and the designative constancy of categories and semantic differentiations for all the members of a society, in that it collectively stabilises the possibilities of concrete reference by means of semiotic materialities (signs).

Collective knowledge is 'passed on' to new members of a society via processes of socialisation. It becomes collectively effective by virtue of the operative fiction that everybody expects everybody else to possess basically the same kind of knowledge. The previously introduced basic pattern of *reflexivity* is at work here, which, with regard to knowledge, we call expectation-expectation, and with regard to motives, intentions and action-orientations of moral judgment, imputation-imputation. Collective knowledge, which is reflexively generated and becomes selectively effective, is continually created anew by agents through processes of conscious activity; it is not simply available for retrieval as a sort of thesaurus of stored information. The operative fiction of collective knowledge may, therefore, indeed be hazardous for individual agents (they may misjudge the knowledge of others), but it is socially most efficient: by virtue of this fiction, the dilemma of the incompatibility of the cognitive autonomy of distinction-setting systems with the social control or orientation of the interactive dependency of suppositions and presuppositions in interactions and communications, is dissolved — one need not know, it is enough to successfully intend. And this must suffice simply because we cannot look into the heads of our fellow-humans.

Models of reality systematise the social interactions of agents with all the domains of action and reference that are considered important for practical life, especially

- with environments and all their relevant resources and properties;
- with agents in their environments, who are important partners in interactions;
- with arrangements of socialisation (institutions, organisations), i.e. with all socially controlled or constrained possibilities of action that are accepted or endured by agents;
- with emotions and their status, expressions, demands and restrictions;

- with moral orientations (values) that are presumed/ expected, admitted or prohibited.

This enumeration is not to suggest that there are no close links between these five central domains of action and reference: any confrontation with the environment is accompanied by more or less conscious emotions and moral orientations, as is any interaction with agents or operation within institutions. There is emotion in morality, just as there is morality in emotion; there is a socialisation of emotion, just as there is emotion in socialisation etc.

The particular importance of these five domains may be justified in the following way. For their constitution as well as the maintenance of their identity, systems must be capable of determining the differences system/environment (environment) and system/system (agent) in a *system-specific* manner; furthermore, they must be able to define their own constraints on possible actions within structures of interaction (patterns of socialisation). In agent-agent relations there has to be continual mutual evaluation of the actions of the partners (morality); and the fact that human systems are body-bound, makes emotions inevitably permanent attractors for all kinds of action (emotion).

It stands to reason, therefore, that all the relevant categories and semantic differentiations, which go to make up a model of reality, are affectively and morally charged. I further assume that they are always more or less automatically 'co-tested' for their (empractical) relevance to practical life, whenever they are employed in suppositions, which will in turn re-adjust their affective and moral charges. As it does not really make sense to envisage a model of reality as a neutral and internally disordered entity, we will have to assume that categories and semantic differentiations are weighted with regard to their social significance (e.g. by means of the difference central/peripheral or dispensable /indispensable), that they can be interlinked with a variable number of other categories and semantic differentiations, and that they are subject to diverse conditions of validity and change. Both the weighting and the charging of categories and differentiations are not carried out anew in every single positing act by agents making use of them. They are probably better thought of as already routinely pre-determined by the partial 'acquisition' of the societal reality model, which is guided by the logic of supposition and presupposition, anyway. In any action, agents presuppose the social reality model as a frame of sense orientation, and affirm it with every successful supposition. Thus the reality model of a society can be modelled as the unity of the difference between categories and semantic differentiations. The model of reality must necessarily be presupposed as (fictitiously because untestably) valid for all members of the society, so that agents may, in situation-specific operations of distinction, 'make sense' by reference to this model and communicate such sense socially by means of linguistic references.

3
Culture Programmes

Models of reality as unities of the difference between categories and semantic differentiations contain those possibilities of semantic/descriptive differentiation with which a society can operate in the five central dimensions named above. Models of reality, as models *for* possible realities, are described here as structure-oriented, i.e. static, semantic networks. They become operative in action only when there is a programme that permits the socially prescribed realisation of potential forms of reference to categories and semantic differentiations as concrete suppositions of distinction, i.e. that permits situation-specific selections from amongst the possible relations between suppositions and presuppositions. These concrete realisations again combine cognitive, affective, and moral components. As selections such suppositions of distinction are contingent; and this contingency is inevitable because every supposition simultaneously demands and admits of the choice of a particular option against the sense-constitutive background of all the excluded possibilities.

The programme of societally practised or expected references to models of reality, i.e. references to categories and semantic differentiations, their affective charge and moral weighting, and equally the programme of admissible orientations in and by the model of reality of a society, I shall call *culture*. It obeys the principle that the consciousness of the agents links itself to culture as the dynamic arrangement for references to models of reality, and that it thus enacts itself.

This train of thought makes clear that models of reality and culture programmes can only be envisaged in strict complementarity. As all categories could in principle be connected with all categories (an ontological exclusion rule is not in sight), we need rules of selection and combination as well as criteria of compatibility in the form of a culture programme, which effect a permanent reduction of the multitude of relations and thus produce given realities as contingent selections out of infinite diversity. It is only as the unity of the difference between contingent selection and infinite diversity of observables and unobservables that a given reality gains processual identity.

Culture as a programme must be construed as inaccessible to learning in every single act of application as it otherwise could not perform any obligatory orientation for agents, nevertheless as quite capable of learning in the long run, because the programme can be (consciously or unconsciously) re-adjusted and changed *reflexively* through the observation and evaluation of the results of its application. Metaphorically we might say that culture is the energy that 'gets' the 'machine' of reality production 'going' by simultaneously distinguishing and combining the stabilisation (tradition) and destabilisation (development) of possibilities of problem-solving. The working of this 'machine' in/through cognitive systems, as a rule, proceeds unthinkingly as an endless process of reshuffling references, i.e. of linking and evaluating semantic categories and differentiations within the context of operations of distinction, that produces in the histories and discourses of agents what they experience as sense (see chapter 5).

Sense can, in the context of this course of reasoning, be described as the permanent experience of the success of culture programmes, or as the socially successful management of *differentiation and distinction* by agents, as purposeful action in a semantic space that must be presupposed for every supposition if sense experience and sense attribution for individual agents are to remain at all possible, socially transferable and compatible. Sense is therefore a difference-free category for N. Luhmann or, in the present context of reasoning, a self-presupposing category that is implicitly contained in every supposition whether one refers to it reflexively or not. We simply cannot imagine doing anything that is not in some way or other observed with the help of the category 'sense'.

However, sense must also be 'made' by way of an arrangement of references. This means that sense is not proposed here as an all-grounding basic category but as the both presupposed and concomitant interpretation of the process of supposition and presupposition.

*

The metaphor of 'distinction management' must briefly be clarified in order to rid it of possible technomorphic associations. We know from history how strongly constellations of power can be determined by the power-charge of differences. Scholars in Cultural Studies have demonstrated how forcefully racism and colonialism were driven by discriminatory discourses. The anglophone discourse of feminism has argued that women had 'no voice' in discourse for so long precisely because the category man was only theoretically understood as the unity of the difference man/woman, but in actual practice was identified with human being + male, — with all its well-known consequences.

An apparently outlandish example, the controversy about apparent death towards the end of the 18th century, makes clear how tangibly the socially practised management of differentiation and distinction with regard to alive/dead can affect entire societal domains of action. Whereas the Jews in Germany had to bury their dead on the day following the incidence of death for religious reasons, the Christians waited for up to a week with the burial because, in the wake of a painstaking medical dispute of reliable features of death, they wanted to await the onset of decomposition so as to be safe from burying an only apparently dead body. It is not difficult to imagine what consequences such difference management had for all the required religious and social activities.

*

These deliberations about culture as a programme were intended to make clear that 'culture', in the theoretical scenario under discussion, does not feature as an observable entity 'existing as an object'. Culture as a programme realises itself in concrete actions, as performed by agents in the form of *offers of options and schematisations of options* for purposes of reference to the model of reality, which is valid for all the agents of a society, who make use of precisely these functions and expect all the other agents to proceed *grosso modo* likewise. Such offers and schematisations may be modified; but any new design will again work as a *prescription* — in keeping with the logic of the culture programme. As a programme for the creation of orderly arrangements and references, which solidifies itself in orderly arrangements and references and *qua* reflexivity functions as an operative fiction integrating cognitive autonomy and social orientation, culture programmes serve as generating mechanisms for all the phenomena that the agents of a society characterise *as cultural phenomena* in the broadest sense. In a nutshell: without the functioning of the culture programme in situation-specific actions of agents, nobody could know what cultural phenomena 'are', how they are recognised and evaluated.

There are two aspects here that need special emphasis. Firstly, culture programmes may become highly differentiated in the course of their evolution, so that speaking of the culture programme of a society can be interpreted to mean the unity of the difference between its sub- or partial programmes (particularly in functionally differentiated societies). Secondly, one must remain aware that agents can, at best, execute, observe and describe only small sections of the culture programme of a society – 'the culture' is thus a *discourse fiction*. In other words, 'there is' no culture as a sum of phenomena, but we need it as a programme in order to be able to generate, observe and evaluate cultural phenomena. Every theory of culture is therefore necessarily a form of cultural practice (i.e. programme application), and descriptions of culture always indicate cultures of description. Every observation of 'culture' is, at the same time, a form of *shaping* it by applying the culture programme.

What was stated with regard to consciousness and communication, applies equally to 'culture': culture programmes are the irreducible condition for dealing with culture programmes; it would therefore be illusory to attempt something like a proper, or objective, theory of culture in which all the cultural phenomena of a society could be specified from outside.

*

The emergence of society, consequently, necessarily presupposes the *co-genesis* of reality models and culture programmes, both of which may differentiate themselves through successful referencing practice. Models of reality and culture programmes, however, do not only co-emerge, they form a mutually constitutive *framework of interactive dependencies* in the sense of General System Theory (see Schlosser 1993), towards which all sense operations in a society are directed. Social integration constitutes itself by the reflexive referral of all actions and communications to the framework of interactive dependencies reality-model &culture-programme, when it is being handled by all agents in a socially binding way — however counterfactual the imputation of the relevance of this sort of operative fiction for all the members of the society may be.

The chosen approach helps to make the everyday concept 'society' more precise. *Society* can now be specified as the unity of the difference between model of reality and culture programme. This specification enables us, furthermore, to explicate all talk of the irreducibility, inaccessibility, indescribability etc. of 'society' and of 'culture' in such a way as to categorise what is called 'society' as a *discourse fiction*. This implies that 'society', too, is not designated as an observable entity existing as an independent object. On the contrary, society constantly *realises* itself by way of the actual exploitation of models of reality and culture programmes through agent-specific suppositions and presuppositions.

The *specificity* of a framework of interactive dependencies reality-model&culture-programme lies in *how* categories and semantic differentiations of the model of reality are semantically related, affectively charged, and morally weighted by the culture programme, so that they can serve as presuppositions (sense orientations) for suppositions (distinctions made). Considering all the descriptions of cultures available today, the (identity-constitutive) specificity of such societal frameworks of interactive dependencies does not primarily rest on the models of reality—there seems to be great similarity amongst humans here—but rather on the culture programme. This is why different 'cultures' appear to be so bafflingly comparable and, at the same time, so bafflingly incompatible and inaccessible, as inter- and multicultural experiences and, in the meantime, the process of globalisation, have taught us.

The categories, as units of the difference between semantic differentiations and distinctions, may remain conscious or may be made conscious as a kind of foil *behind* all suppositions. In the observation of the second order, therefore, all the options of the culture programme appear to be contingent due to their selectivity, but also changeable and malleable, if new programme components are successfully implemented as prescriptions and other components are re-valued. Contingency is thus not seen here as groundlessness but as the presupposition for mobility and creativity.

On this basis, 'culture' as culture programme can be put into a twofold perspective:

- as the totality of all those *realised* programme applications at a particular point in time, which are familiar and available for exploitation (tradition);
- as an open horizon of *realisable* alternative programme projects and programme applications (innovation).

The relative difference between these two possibilities of observation specifies, in a sense, the dynamic potential of a culture programme.

The perspective of tradition was interpreted by N. Luhmann to mean that 'culture' is the memory of a society.

This assertion can be made more concrete by stating that the traditions of a society 'preserve' successful problem-solutions in the context of a culture programme, which make important contributions to its identity. The firm conviction of 'we have always done it this way' provides security of action by rendering contingency invisible.

The perspective of innovation may be generally titled 'creativity' or 'vitality', which save culture programmes from trivialisation and rigidity and enable societies to react in a system-specific way to perceived processes of change.

*

The logic of the present argument makes it unthinkable to conceive of a 'society' without 'culture' and of a 'culture' without a 'society'. Both become effective and observable only in the applications and the exploitations of the culture programme through cognitively and communicatively active agents. Without agents, culture programmes would literally *make no sense*. In this way, *all* agents contribute to their 'culture', although they are, in the active implementation of culture programmes, bound by their scope of application. We can thus pin down a specific feature of 'culture': in concrete applications of culture programmes, it can be observed simultaneously as supposition and presupposition, programme and application, prescription and change.

A sharp contraposition of culture programme and action, of symbolic sense orientation and concrete individual action, as suggested by numerous authors, obscures the *framework of their potential generation* (as a causal mode). Actions are certainly always agent-bound, but that does not apply to all the options of sense 'kept in reserve' in the culture programme, with whose help agents can pack into their own and other actions *socially communicable* sense, i.e. are enabled to understand and interpret such actions. These interdependencies will be examined more closely in chapter 5 under the heading histories&discourses.

4

Interim Summary 1

As already stated in the preface, human beings evidently face a basic problem in everything they do or miss: the *relationship between selection and contingency*. At any point in time, we can only realise one of several possibilities, therefore each and every one of our suppositions is selective and, because of the excluded alternatives, contingent. Selectivity and contingency are reciprocally dependent.

Such a hazardous situation needs some kind of control in order to secure the communal life of agents. This means that the treatment of contingency must be regulated in a socially binding way for all socialised agents. Thus the second basic problem of all societal life is also demarcated: the successful *balancing of the inescapability of cognitive autonomy and the necessity of social orientation*.

The first and fundamental solution of this problem has been discussed in the last few chapters: the culture programme of a society must control the admissible references to the model of reality of the society for agents by means of adequate social inescapabilities. Thus the auto-constitutive co-functioning of model of reality and culture programme, within a framework of interactive dependencies, 'treats' universal (non-specific) contingency with the help of specific (selective) contingency. This kind of contingent treatment of contingency functions as the famous blind spot in action and communication. In this way, the observation of the treatment of contingency by means of contingency, which is quite accessible to the observer of the second order, is rendered invisible to agents in histories and discourses (i.e. to observers of the first order) through culture; it is removed from observation — the agents remain action-empowered through the elimination of everything unobservable in their sphere of action. And as every agent tacitly presumes all other agents to operate in the shadow of the same blind spot, a co-orientation through reflexivity of all agents to the same framework of interactive dependencies of model of reality & culture programme becomes possible. Insecurity as the consequence of contingency is transformed into a steadfast system of orientation-orientations through the reflexivity of operative fictions, which reconciles cognitive autonomy and social orientation by making the system-specificity of all suppositions orient itself to fictitiously imputed social possibilities of orientation. In other words, cognitive systems bypass, as it were, the impossibility of controlling each other by direct intervention and, consequently, orient themselves by self-constituted instances of control, which they consider to be socially effective and legitimate. The observation that such self-orientations actually work, automatically renders invisible the contingency of every supposition, which could only be observed by observers of observers. For them, the culture programme, as a rule, provides cultural values which enable them to tolerate the shock of their latent observation (of universal contingency), e.g. values like wisdom or prudence, equanimity, humour, tolerance of relativity, or a 'sense of the possible' (following R. Musil). But it is only too well known that even second-order observers cannot escape the contingency dilemma that expresses itself in the hierarchisation of observation:

Interim Summary 1

even the observers of the second and third (and higher) orders have their blind spots—but it is just these which enable them to see something at all. Rendering contingency invisible is, therefore, the fundamental presupposition of our experience of reality, and this experience does not at all lack certainty, because it pervades the actual present as we experience it.

5
Histories & Discourses

According to our experience of life, all our actions and communications are woven into interdependent previous and subsequent actions and communications. These interdependencies do not, however, integrate just arbitrary actions and communications in our environment, but only those to which we (can) relate. With regard to the totality of all actions and communications in a society, such interdependencies are highly selective and acquire meaningful coherence and identity through the supposition of difference — it is this particular interdependency here and now, and no other, that concerns me. Such selectivity facilitates possible interconnections and thus necessarily leads to the emergence of external and internal arrangements that allow for the synthesis of actions and communications of and for agents, and pave the way for possibilities to communicate them through the reflexive reference to relevant interdependencies. Communicability, on the other hand, socially endorses this synthesis — not least because such communications make use of conventionalised narrative schemata, and are realised in the typified frames of particular genres.

In other words, the selectivity of reference to actions and communications in our environment and the possibility of reflexive reference to this selectivity, by the logic of its own procedure, generates action- and communication-related symbolic ordering mechanisms that I shall henceforth term 'histories' and 'discourses'.[1]

*

By *history* I understand a configuration of action sequences of an agent, arranged according to a category of meaning (from meaningful to meaningless). Histories arise through the intrinsic concatenation or interweaving of actions so as to make every action, as the supposition of presuppositions, the presupposition for subsequent actions, and so on. Agents never set out presupposition-free, they always continue with suppositions on the 'plafond' of manifold presuppositions.

All agents live their histories, and live within their histories of histories, i.e. in configurations of action sequences which they themselves have consciously arranged, or which have been more or less arranging themselves during their practice of life, and which have been synthesised into meaningful histories by the agents' relating of the histories to themselves — for nobody else could do that or would at all be interested in doing it. Our histories connect with our own histories but may also connect with the histories of other agents if a common interpretation can possibly be utilised. In this case, several agents may live a *partially* shared history for a certain length of time, which will, however, never be identical for any of them.

Our own histories can, therefore, be specified as unities of the difference between our own histories and the histories of others, i.e. of histories that we experience ourselves, and

---

[1] My deliberations on 'histories' take up some of the stimulating ideas of the phenomenologist and legal philosopher Wilhelm Schapp, who has, sadly enough, been practically forgotten, without incorporating en bloc his *Philosophie der Geschichten* (1953/1959).

other histories that we have somehow been made acquainted with.

Our histories 'are' whatever we find ourselves in, or more precisely: whatever we project ourselves into, whenever we reflexively refer to possible interdependencies of our actions, and try to place and interpret ourselves by virtue of such reference. This is why the synthesis of histories is of great importance for the formation of our identity (see chapter 11). Histories do not last for ever, we much rather let them arise. They are the products of reflexion, continually generated afresh, and never identical for all those enmeshed in them. Only those 'enmeshed in histories' — thus the canonical formulation by W. Schapp — are capable of developing the belief that something similar to their own history 'exists', and that they are able to communicate information about it.

Histories are modelled here as meaningful dynamic patterns of order of, and for, references, which permit the establishing of relations. Solely through such relations may actions emerge as *compact interpretative moulds* for meaningful events or happenings. Actions are always part of a sequence of actions. Histories are always part of a meaning-determined sequence of histories, even though they may sometimes appear meaningless. Histories proceed from histories and merge into other histories. Strictly speaking, we would have to say that histories, too, like actions or processes of consciousness, 'are nothing else', and that means: cannot be experienced in any other way than as *transitions* the continuity of which we (counterfactually) interrupt in thinking or communicating, in order to make them observable and describable *qua* structure formation, while they keep moving on. Observables (discontinuity) and unobservables (continuity) are strictly complementary (S. Jünger 2002: 45).

Only by way of creating discontinuity, i.e. by interrupting processes, can we achieve structure formation (observations, reflexive differentiations) that permits us to disregard dynamics.

Two conclusions can be drawn from the considerations presented:

- Histories are products of reflection and discourse, which arise through reference as syntheses of event sequences.
- Reflexive operations in consciousness and thinking require narrative schematisations (communication patterns); the creation of histories is, therefore, closely connected with communication. The self-communication of consciousness and thinking as well as interactive communication presuppose communication patterns of various kinds and continually endorse them by communicative success. In other words, cognition necessarily requires linguistic and communicative arrangements for its own processing.

The upshot is then: histories and discourses 'are' the factors that block my retreat just as beginnings and endings. From histories and discourses one can only move into other histories and discourses, and this transition is experienced and interpreted as a special framework of interactively dependent histories and discourses.

*

W. Schapp rightly emphasises that histories are not comprehended but *interpreted*. Here again first-order observation must be distinguished from observation of the second order. For the agents enmeshed in histories, their interpretation of actions is the mode of realisation of their histories. For the observer of a history or for agents observing a history in retrospect, interpreting observation is realised as another kind of framework of interdependent histories. Observer and observed live different histories and discourses that must not be confused. Therefore, the question of the correctness of an interpretation is not an abstract and principled one, but always takes the form of opening and performing another history in which observer and observed are now (partially) enmeshed together so as to assess the quality and acceptance of the interpretation by way of feedback loops. Observation is, therefore, never neutral or objectively derivable but always a co-enmeshed, participant, and involved process. — The box-stage model of observation was already discarded ironically by Heinz von Foerster long ago.

Histories govern the selective reference to our environment (and our environment 'is' nothing but the systemic framework of our environmental contacts) by recognisably exploiting the difference to other histories. In other words, our histories are differentially related to the totality of all those other histories, which we notice or observe in our own histories and which we have been made acquainted with in some way or other.

Histories result from coping with a double reference, namely self-reference and other-reference. We experience our histories as unities of the difference between our own history and other histories, between experienced and unexperienced histories. Thus the unity of the difference between our own history and other histories for us forms the mode of the givenness or availability of reality and society.

*

As explained above, histories cannot be imagined without communication. Our communications are equally interdependent — temporally, formally, and thematically. The circulation of knowledge realises itself as the permanent transition from suppositions to presuppositions to suppositions to presuppositions, and so on.

The selection patterns for the internal ordering of our communications within given histories, which are specified thematically and formally (syntax, stylistics, metaphors, forms of genres, patterns of presentation, and the like), I shall call *discourse*. Like histories, discourses result from the handling of self-reference and other-reference, which is itself determined by the difference between contributions and themes. Discourses select those contributions which are thematically and formally connectible according to their internal logic and the social positioning of the discourses in question, and they synthesise them to a meaningful communication process in such a way as to admit only thematically and formally adequate contributions. In this way, discourses select not only contributions but also contributors. Not every agent can take part in every discourse, access may be socially defined or left to chance — only inscribed students can take part in a seminar with a limited number of participants, but practically any visitor to a pub may join in a conversation at the bar.

The specific character of the discourses which in their totality embody the order of the communication system of a society, constitutes both their contingency and their identity. Universal contingency is, however, rendered invisible for individual participants in communication because, being enmeshed in quite specific discourses, they are exempt from any reflection on why they do not participate in others. The discourses in which we actively participate also stand in a relation of difference to the discourses with which we are not mixed-up or into which we are not drawn.

The selectivity of our discourse participations can therefore be utilised for our identity management. (Tell me what discourses you are enmeshed in, and I shall tell you who you socially 'are'.)

*

Our histories and discourses (or: discourse participations) are related to each other, or 'stacked into each other', as it were. Discourse participations realise themselves in histories, histories are the subjects of discourses, and vice versa. Histories and discourses in their totality form a complementary framework of interactive dependencies of their own, which may be observed from two perspectives: as history (action framework), or as discourse (communication framework). To mark this complementarity optically, I shall notate this framework of interactive dependencies as histories&discourses. The internal order of histories&discourses results from the orientation of our actions and communications towards the 'superordinate', as the more abstract framework of interactive dependencies reality model&culture programme. In this perspective society can, consequently, be described as the unity of the differences between the histories&discourses of the society members, i.e. all the agents accepting and practising this culturally controlled arrangement of references.

*

The interweaving of both these processual frameworks becomes apparent when the *components* of histories&discourses are more closely examined, namely actions and communications (more details below). Actions as agent-based processes are realised as instantiations of *action-schemata* from the repertoire of reality models&culture programmes which, as societally conventionalised schemata (or: as operative fictions of the collective expectation of collective expectations), define the type of meaning regarding the particular action in question. Actions are, as it were, performed, 'read' and interpreted according to the instructions of the action-schema. Such 'reading' synthesises the temporal sequence of elementary events into a particular action (opening, and not painting, a window).

Actions can thus be subjected to a twofold observation: one directed at the sequence of the processes or operations taking place, the other directed at the order-supplying patterns of coherence of these processes within the frame of meaning of a particular action-schema.

Consequently, all the actions that I am enmeshed in or that I have been made acquainted with, form the histories-component of my framework of interactive dependencies histories&discourses.

Communications, too, realise themselves in the mode of reference to communication-schemata that pre-orient, as operative fictions, the way the communication (component) is read. Communications are enacted, they need time, and they take place within frameworks of action. All the communications that I am enmeshed in or that I have been made acquainted with, form the discourses-component of my framework of interactive dependencies histories&discourses.

While we may intuitively think that our histories are directly and completely 'ours', because we tend to disregard the necessity of the social corroboration of our actions, we are necessarily co-enmeshed in discourses because communications evidently require communication partners.

Three aspects of histories and discourses may be distinguished by *temporalising* observation: histories&discourses, as an expectation-oriented framework of interactive dependencies, encompasses the *presuppositions* for everything that takes place in histories and discourses (and, according to the argument developed here, all human life takes place in histories and discourses). Histories&discourses realise themselves in the form of *processes* that are understood and evaluated by means of the difference history/discourse; and histories&discourses are always the *result* of presupposition-rich processes, which themselves become the presuppositions of subsequent histories and discourses.

This line of argument further includes the assumption that histories and discourses are not mutually related by some mode of mapping or representation but by a mode of *adjustment to each other*. This condition must be fulfilled as one of the fundamental expectations connected with histories and discourses if agents are to find them satisfying — the criteria for the fit naturally being as diverse as histories and discourses themselves.

*

It must be emphasised that the manoeuvre to begin with histories and discourses does in no way entail any meta-processual ontological presumptions. It merely makes use of the by now familiar mechanism of supposition and presupposition, which implies that every supposition — whether as action, thought or description — necessarily takes place at a particular point in time and in a particular situation and rests on two presuppositions: the presupposition of preceding suppositions (in order to exclude postulating an absolute beginning), and the presupposition of the unity of the difference between categories and semantic differentiations (so as to exclude claiming the creation of absolute meaning). As operative processes and as producers of meaning, suppositions are only possible in the presupposition-context of histories&discourses — or whatever one chooses to call these two components of the framework of interactive dependencies. It acquires its basic significance because within it the meaning potential of its necessarily always presupposed framework of interactive dependencies model of reality&culture programme is actually exploited in an agent- and situation-specific manner. The ordering potential of model of reality&culture programme can only turn into empirically relevant directives by virtue of the ordering patterns for actions and communications in histories&discourses.

The difference history/discourse can be re-visited on either side of this distinction. The unity of the differences history/discourse and discourse/history secures the identity of histories&discourses. To put it differently: histories&discourses is seen as a complex dynamic framework of interactive dependencies that safeguards the unity of the difference process/sense-orientation (or process/structure-formation). The framework of interactive dependencies histories&discourses should not, therefore, be understood as a mere aggregate of components. On the contrary, it integrates in a communicable way, both empirically and conceptually, memories, expectations and experiences as well as feeling, knowing and evaluating, both empirically and conceptually for every agent.

Histories and discourses provide patterns of expectation and interpretation for the feelings and experiences of agents and thus circumscribe their possibilities of association. Histories and discourses arise from, and persist through, relationality and reflexivity — without reference no effect and no communicability. They are structurally coupled to each other, both complementary and cooperative, thereby increasing their complexity. Histories are enmeshed in histories, discourses in discourses. Histories are enmeshed in discourses and discourses in histories.

Histories and discourses integrate language and life forms (according to L. Wittgenstein). They represent all that agents can achieve by action, knowledge and communication (with fuzzy edges), and incorporate the realities of agents. Histories and discourses are instruments of coupling, embodiment and emergence — depending on observation and description. In the framework of interactive dependencies of histories&discourses collective knowledge is built up, which must be continually constructed and used afresh by agents according to social rules in each and every cognitive process — knowledge is action. This knowledge, reflexively (and fictitiously) ascribed by all interacting agents, on the one hand, provides for the integration of agents in histories&discourses, and allows, on the other hand, the sufficiently solid integration of agent-bound histories and discourses 'in society'. Contrary to the traditional separation of individual and society, the histories&discourses idea offers the possibility of speaking of one closed framework of interactive dependencies with two *observation options for each* component level: agent/society, process/structure, consciousness/communication, all these pairs of components being complementary.

'Enmeshedness' in histories&discourses furthermore describes a basic condition (= for agents an empirically ascertainable place outside histories&discourses is unimaginable because the reflection of this basic condition itself cannot but take place in a framework of histories&discourses) as much as a precarious relationship between freedom and enmeshedness. We can choose to become enmeshed in certain histories&discourses, we have no choice with regard to others. In addition, there is broad variation with regard to the accessibility of our enmeshedness to conscious control and corresponding obligations. For this reason observers can and will usually assess our 'enmeshedness' quite differently from ourselves. This means that even in partially shared and interpreted histories system-specificity remains uncancellable, as is only too well-known to members of families who, despite many commonalities, never manage to be 'of one mind'.

*

If we are enmeshed in histories&discourses that themselves refer to the framework of interactive dependencies of reality model&culture programme, if, to put it differently, all our suppositions are constituted by presuppositions that we as agents can never catch up with, then it is clear that we will always arrive *too late*. Our brain must already have done its work before something can reach our consciousness; we need to have acquired linguistic competence before we can become aware of speaking a language; in order to realise that we live in a 'culture' we must already be capable of applying parts of a culture programme; we can only experience our present in the present that we can only describe as a forgotten past, and so on. This reflection once again endorses the rejection of any possibility of a presupposition-free beginning. And it also endorses the rejection of any probability of subject-independent knowledge and the accessibility of objective truth. No human being can open innocent eyes, i.e. unaffected by the contingent conditions of the possibility of their actions.

To emphasise it once more: histories and discourses are not postulated here as the prime foundations on which to erect a theory systematically. Nor are we involved in a start-up manoeuvre of the kind 'histories and discourses exist!' The concepts 'history' and 'discourse' much rather serve to synthesise descriptively lifeworld experiences whose plausibility cannot reasonably be questioned, because they specify the presuppositions of these very experiences. Only in contexts of communication can we assert or describe something as something, as is happening here right now, although — as J. Mitterer keeps pointing out — the object of the description must not be separated from the description of the object if dualisms are to be avoided. Only in sequences of connected actions can we bring about transitions from *a* to *b*, from *before* to *after*, or from *because* to *therefore*, and experience and describe them as actions of a particular type. The considerations presented here are, therefore, not concerned with asserting the existence or non-existence of histories and discourses, but exclusively with what can be achieved with the help of these concepts in discourses, and what further connections may be established.

And the discourses of observers can, of course, never involve themselves with whether histories and discourses are described correctly or wrongly; this would imply that our descriptions were intended to apprehend them as something existing in a 'world beyond discourse' (according to J. Mitterer). Instead, these concepts seek to fixate the thought terminologically that only the enactment of suppositions makes something happen for us, that these suppositions have presuppositions and consequences, and that we require practical and semantic arrangements for the meaningful handling of suppositions and presuppositions, which enable us to derive from mere sequences of events socially communicable frameworks in the form of actions and communications. From this perspective, the task of histories and discourses is to process contingency through contingency on their specific level of synthesis, by having agents exploit socially viable opportunities for meaning creation with regard to experiences, actions and communications, with reference to the framework of interactive dependencies of reality model&culture programme.

Thus the logic of supposition and presupposition compels us to accept a framework of interactive dependencies histories&discourses as an ordering instrument for concrete suppositions of all kinds. The contingent arrangements of given histories and discourses cognitively and communicatively obscure universal contingency, and they lend so much life-practical support to specific ways of coping with contingency that agents may lead a successful life and society can go on functioning.

6
Agency

In the preceding deliberations on histories and discourses, histories have been modelled theoretically as modes of the order-creating synthesis of actions from amongst sequences of events. The concept of action has not yet been explained in detail although it belongs to the fundamental concepts of the theoretical scenario developed here. This will be rectified now in what follows.

*

The elementary form of all our references, as based upon the fundamental mechanism of supposition (operative aspect) and presupposition (sense orientation), I call *action*. Being tied to this fundamental mechanism, all action is 'enmeshed' in the complementary framework of selection and contingency: we do this and not something else, and we do it in this way, although another way is also conceivable. The contingency of our actions is 'treated' by means of *schematisation*, which assigns individual events to particular action types. Action types are made available to us through the culture programme. As with all other sense orientations, we assume with regard to action types that we share their knowledge with others: 'One knows' how to shop, how to travel by bus, or how to pour wine. Schema knowledge belongs among the elementary operative fictions that help us to treat contingency in the framework of interactive dependencies of histories&discourses and allow us to acquire self-confidence in action, something that can only be shaken by observations of the second order.

Action realises itself as the synthesis of the *transitions* from one event to the next. (A person pulls the hand out of the coat pocket, moves it to the hat, raises the hat: a formal act of greeting has been carried out.) For such synthesis, action schemata provide meaningful interrupters of contingency that transform actions into compact socially relevant forms, as it were. (If a greeting partner is in sight, observers will not interpret the act of greeting as an airing of the scalp, as driving off flies, or as a neurotic tick of the hat-bearer.)

Through this mode, action is necessarily connected with *time and space*; for although actions can be described as syntheses of events *qua* subsumption under typifying schemata, they can only be envisaged as taking place in temporally concrete situations. As operative fictions, they must be ascribed by the agents themselves as well as by others as this or that particular action. Here again the mode expounded by S. Jünger applies: sequences of events, as uninterrupted transitions, can only be made discontinuous, and thus be structured as actions of a particular kind, through consciously reflexive observations and descriptions.

In these complicated frameworks, agency — besides identity as a function of attributed action coherence — shows itself to be closely connected with other results of manoeuvres of reflexivity, e.g. with morality and truth. Agency is connected with identity in that the observed self-assessment by others is balanced with personal self-assessment (see chapter 11), with morality in that any form of reference to other agents is evaluated with regard to moral principles of orientation (see chapter 12), and with truth in that any form of action-governing knowledge is automatically (co-)tested for its truth (see chapter 13).

*

In what follows, these abstract introductory reflections that were, first and foremost, intended to recapitulate the key figures of the reasoning presented so far, will be elucidated in greater detail.

With regard to the aforementioned problem of *schemata*, the following ought to be noted: one of the most famous formulae introduced into systems theory by N. Luhmann is the 'reduction of complexity'. On closer scrutiny, this formula implies a dualist epistemology that takes an objective amount of complexity in the environment of systems for granted, and then focuses on the ways and means that systems can employ to reduce the surplus of complexity to a measure they can control. In the non-dualist conception developed here, this argument must practically be reversed. Systems do not *reduce* complexity, but much rather through their operation *generate* system-specific and system-compatible complexity. Schemata and schematisations play a double role in this. On the one hand, they relieve cognitive and communicative processes of otherwise requisite operations of synthesis and observations of control (and so accelerate these processes considerably); on the other hand, they allow for sociability due to the concurrent evaluation of schemata as socially relevant patterns of order, although the agents can only operate in a strictly system-specific manner (as indicated by the formula of 'cognitive autonomy'). Cognitive and communicative schemata are not at all meant to reduce discovered or known complexity schematically (and thus, from a dualist point of view, to distort it), but to constitute complexity, in the first place, in that the active systems in question make their means of reality-construction work in a histories&discourses-specific way.

As mentioned at the beginning, we cannot, strictly speaking, observe *actions,* but only sequences of events or processes involving agents in histories&discourses, which we, as observers, more or less automatically subsume under a particular action-schema and consequently assess *as* this or that action. Everything we cover with these concepts necessarily results from our distinctions; 'agency' must therefore be construed as an *observer category.* (Whoever does not know that the raising of a hat means carrying out a formal act of greeting, will find it difficult to synthesise the sequence of events described above.) Action is ascribed to agents, in the form of self-ascription or other-ascription. Such ascription has sense and function, it is desirable or undesirable, acceptable or unacceptable, it may succeed or fail. It is part of the framework of praise or blame, recognition or rejection, reward or punishment, in histories and discourses. Action cannot be separated from action bearers nor from affective, moral and empractical assessment. Actions are, therefore, from the perspective of both agents and observers, 'interpretation constructs' (in the understanding of H. Lenk), which need not at all be identical, perhaps cannot ever be identical, because the agent and the observer of the agent are enmeshed in different histories or live different histories.

*

The observational variation sense-orientation/process thus yields the result that there must be a clear distinction between actions as processes in time and space and action-schemata as sense-schemata, as well as between endo- and exo-observations and interpretations of whatever is seen or lived as a particular kind of action. In both observational perspectives the themes of *intentionality* and *action-rationality* play quite different roles. The observers of an action are primarily interested in the intentions of agents so as to be able to fit their observations into action-schemata and action-expectations of their own. The agents, however, primarily want to cope successfully with situations, or solve problems in ways that correspond or *can* be connected with intentions that either become apparent during their actions or are constructed subsequently. Agents, through their actions, want to achieve effects; observers are out for understanding and want to find the attribution-schemata within which the observable actions of agents make sense *for them* as observers. Agents, when acting, are only aware of their actions and the kinds of action they are realising, insofar as they are able to inform themselves or others about them, i.e. insofar they are able or wish to make their actions communicatively connectible through reflexive discontinuation.

*

Assuming that actions as *tokens* of *types* happen within the framework of interactive dependencies of histories&discourses, one may also very well assume that agents act in histories&discourses *with such good reasons* as have evolved through preceding experiences and knowledge constructions in their histories&discourses. Actions are not explained through natural causes, i.e. causally, but in the light of previously made, and on the basis of action-schemata expectable, *experiences* that also orient the *expectations* related to the actions to be undertaken here and now. This is why actions should not *only* be described or explained according to schemata of rationality, causality, strategic problem-solving, intentionality or the realisation of motives, although all these instances are important and should not be neglected. It is also a question of the degree of trivialisation of actions and the appropriate framework of histories&discourses, which of these schemata is to play a role to what degree, with what kind, what required measure of conscious control, and finally, on what level of observability.

As has already been said, action-schemata carry affective and moral aspects that agents may be differently aware of — as always with schemata. The decision, therefore, what a particular action means, is not a question of a state of consciousness or of subjective feelings and evaluations, but a question of the histories&discourses-specific assessment of a *schema* that cannot be changed by arbitrary interpretation. The reference to such schemata, which is reflexively attributed to other agents, achieves the reconciliation of cognitive autonomy and social orientation in the sphere of action.

*

These considerations indicate, as P. Janich emphasises, that agency must be learned in the frames of meaning production within action-schemata by way of cultural programming. They make clear, furthermore, that actions, histories and discourses form a systemic framework: only within the meaning-producing framework of histories&discourses, oriented by the framework of interactive dependencies of reality model&culture programme, do individual agents become cognitively empowered to act (by virtue of contingency being rendered invisible), and their actions become socially interpretable (by subsumption under schemata). As actions have to be corroborated as particular meaningful actions by others, agency necessarily imposes the difference alter/ego.

Furthermore, the execution of an action must not be confused with the appearance of a desired result. Actions may have desired and intended *results*, but also most certainly unwanted *consequences*. (One goes on holiday by car, safely reaches the hotel — but the following morning the car has been stolen.)

The general principle is: no action without knowledge, no knowledge without action. Action leads to knowing, knowing to ability embodied in connected actions. The intrinsic interdependence of action, knowing/understanding, and ability, which — due to human bodyhood — always involves cognitive, affective and moral components as attractors, defines what and how we come to know. That perceiving, describing, knowing and talking are actions must, therefore, never be overlooked. Perception, too, is a kind of praxis that is culturally programmed and that can only be split up analytically into separately describable bodily and mental aspects. The interface between agent and reality should, therefore, not be located in perceptions, knowledge or language, but in the active embodiments of perceiving, knowing, and communicating within the concrete framework of interactive dependencies of histories&discourses.

What is *social* about human action, it has been argued so far, is not the subjective meaning of actions, but the collectively effective, culturally programmed, variety of knowledge-controls, which bring about the reconciliation of cognitive autonomy and social orientation through an obligatory order of references, for which natural language, and all the media since the rise of writing, have played a decisive role.[1] It becomes apparent again that supposition

---

[1] As explained in various places, I conceive of language not as a medium but as an instrument of communication. Media — beginning with writing — I understand as a compact concept systemically integrating four component-domains:

and presupposition, sense-orientation and process-orientation, are observational variants and not 'real alternatives' that can be interpreted dualistically. Actions without agents are, according to this reasoning, as unthinkable as actions without sense-producing social schemata of interpretation, which must be used by agents as collective knowledge if they intend to act in a socially relevant manner.

The concept 'agent' can thus be modelled theoretically as the unity of the difference between cognitive autonomy and social orientation, which embodies itself in actions and communications within histories&discourses.

- communication instruments such as language and images,
- sets of technical implements (from pen and paper to internet technology),
- the social-systemic organisation of the exploitation of these implements (e.g. scriptoria, publishing or broadcasting houses),
- the media offers resulting from the combined action of these components.

7

Communication

At the beginning of this chapter, I shall, as before, first briefly review the general frame of the argument developed so far, in which the following deliberations on communication will then be assigned to their proper place.

Like all other activities, communication — however it may be characterised in specific detail — realises itself as a supposition in a framework of presuppositions. *Qua* supposition it is defined as action (operative aspect) whose presuppositions are specified as sense components of the framework of interactive dependencies reality model&culture programme. Communications as actions occur, or are enacted and meaningfully oriented, in the framework of interactive dependencies histories&discourses in spatiotemporally defined specific histories and discourses.

As an auto-constitutive framework of suppositions and presuppositions, communication, too, is subject to the complementarity of selection and contingency. And as a fundamental societal operation (without communication no socialisation), communication contributes in a special way to the socially mandatory treatment of contingency, which empowers agents to social action despite their cognitive autonomy. Here again schematisations play a central role, and there is evidently a rich diversity of schematisations that can be observed in the sphere of communication, from phonetics through grammar to forms of genre, discourse, and further macro-forms.

From its origins to its applications, communication can be described as a prime example of functional reflexivity. Born of reflexive perception which, by the formation of expectation-expectations and imputation-imputations, makes social action possible, communication thrives on the basis of the operative fiction that certain semantic sets of knowledge, motivational situations, and evaluation routines, can be presumed to be binding collective knowledge for all partners in action. Taking into account the cognitive autonomy (i.e. the strict system-specificity of all suppositions) of agents, communication cannot, as many authors have already demonstrated, be modelled as the transfer of information because information can only arise through system-specific suppositions (in the all-too famous heads of agents). It is much rather plausible to construe communication as orientation-orientation (according to G. Rusch 1999), i.e. again as a reflexive process, in which communication partners offer each other orientation that can be taken up in system-specific ways. The degree of consensual exploitation, according to this description, depends on how unanimously the partners (can) adduce collective knowledge, and how schematised the modalities of such exploitations are in particular types of situation. Communication, as the common reference to reflexively attributed presuppositions, engenders the expectation of understanding, which is inherent in all communication as its intended success.

Evidently, the framework of interactive dependencies histories&discourses plays an important role for communication; it builds up the frameworks of experience and expectation, which have evolved in the history of histories&discourses of every agent, as directories of selection for imminent selections: agents may have to act contingently but they do not at all have to act capriciously. Agents naturally participate only in certain discourses, but not without good reasons. And the orientation by such directories relieves agents of the neuroticising relentless reflection on why they do A and not B to Z, and why they talk about Alpha and not about Beta to Omega.

*

Three thematic areas have been introduced in this brief summary, which play an important role in every theory of communication, i.e. the themes of cognition and communication, of communication and culture, and of communication, communication instruments, and media. A few comments only on all this.

Paul Valéry once noted pithily: 'Language has never come face to face with thought.' In other words, cognition and communication operate in different domains and in different modes, and therefore the assumption of a direct translation from one to the other is not deemed plausible. Although orientation offers may be used in both domains for domain-specific operations — texts and media products may be turned into thoughts and other texts and media products precisely because in both domains collective knowledge is used for the production, reception and processing of texts in comparable ways. (This relationship may be termed 'structural coupling'.) This comparability is guaranteed by the exploitation of the framework of interactive dependencies reality model&culture programme within the framework of interactive dependencies histories&discourses in concrete communications; and all successful exploitation of these fictitiously presupposed frameworks of interactive dependencies stabilises, at the same time, their efficiency and legitimacy. Communication, in its handling of media offers, operates by means of the empowerment mechanism of culture programmes, which can be considered as meaningful only with regard to such social application. Metaphorically one could say: 'Culture conducts communication', and communication imperturbably 'performs' culture programmes. Both make sense only in strict complementarity. And like 'culture', communication, too, is the irreducible presupposition for any involvement with itself.

*

In addition to the presupposition reality model&culture programme in histories&discourses, communication needs *materialities*, in/at which societal experiences can durably condense. In other words, it needs perceptible and semantically functional semiotic instruments of communication. In a histories&discourses-oriented conception of language, two important theoretical decisions with regard to this problem have already been taken: that which is *observable* in communicative actions in histories and discourses, consists in *semiotic materialities* (figures of expression) and not in meanings (cognitive sets of orderly arrangements). Thus, the rule-conformity of their employment, which we presuppose as a meaning-endowing schema-orientation whenever we speak, must lie in the materiality and not (only) in the meanings. This rule-conformity is not only responsible for the socially acceptable concatenation and textual realisation of such semiotic materials, but also for the socially provided scope of their cognitive and communicative processing (= meaning construction), which is established by rigid linguistic socialisation. In its course, agents learn (largely unconsciously) in prototypical and therefore formative situations and through the orientation by persons of trust, when and how such semiotic materials are to be managed (the typical command being: we say it this way/this is called such and such...), and what social experiences are condensed by such materials and their implementation — a typical process of reflexive structure-building from praxis for praxis (according to H. Feilke).

It is an important aspect of the acquisition of a native language, the most fundamental and, at the same time, most complex instrument of communication, that children invariably learn speech in a *living environment*, i.e. in a concrete histories&discourses-framework, and by acquiring language 'acquire' the competence for functioning living environments. Teachers and learners act as observed observers, whose syntheses of behaviour (partially) adjust to each other. Children learn in the socialisation process how the models of reality of their society are built up and what possibilities of action (in the broadest sense, from cognitive to communicative and non-linguistic actions) can be made use of within their social framework. Thus language acquisition, in abstract terms, leads to the acquisition of the individual competence to generate collective language application knowledge (both on the expression and the content plane), whereby this collective knowledge stabilises itself individually and socially through reflexivity along the dimensions of time, facts, and sociability. The operative fiction of collective knowledge, intuitively expected by the normal speaker, is the foundation of the inter-individuality of the processes of cognition and communication.

Semiotic materiality — independent of the individual speaker but socially binding for all speakers — condenses, as it were, the social experiences resulting from its viable handling. Here again we encounter a *reflexive* process: language is the product of speaking and guides speaking in a socially binding manner. Language speaks speech, and speech speaks language. Supposition (speaking) and presupposition (language) are constitutively interlocked, their distinction once again marking observational variance and not ontological duality.

Communication as the realisation of orientation-orientations, profits in quite a special way from the *schematisation gains* achieved by a society. Schematisations have been defined as the fixing of operative fictions that, on the one hand, produce cognitive, communicative, and action implementation routines and thus greater speed, that, on the other hand, create collective sets of knowledge, which make orientation-orientations (more) probable. The more schematisations, the richer the themes, forms and usages of and for communication. Furthermore, these very themes, forms and usages can again be observed and made the topic of communication. In this way, the opportunities multiply to generate significant differences through the creation of differences, i.e. to achieve communication gains by deviating from expectations, which in turn confronts the dominant culture programme with the question as to whether it can interpretatively cope with the deviations—a mechanism gleefully explored by all subcultures.

These histories&discourses-oriented reflections on communication and language not only militate against dualist theories of language but also against *dualist theories of meaning*, which distinguish ontologically between materiality and meaning. Materiality and meaning must, however, be viewed as strictly complementary phenomena. This implies that the distinction materiality/meaning (following the distinction observable/unobservable) only makes sense with regard to the unity of this distinction, namely 'speaking' as communicative action in histories&discourses.

The distinction materiality/meaning thus again symbolises nothing but *observational* alternatives that ought not to be interpreted dualistically as ontological differences (here the realm of purely arbitrary signs, there the realm of ideal meanings). For speakers in histories&discourses there can be no arbitrariness in language. And the arbitrariness of linguistic signs, claimed by second-order observers on the basis of language comparisons, trivially claims nothing more than that Italian is different from Russian.

*

In the philosophy of language and in linguistics there is still active rivalry between *semiotic models* and *action models* of language. According to the argument presented so far, this is an implausible and sterile alternative, because the difference sign/action marks an alternative in observations, not an ontological alternative: 'action' refers to the operative aspect of speaking, 'sign' to the aspect of meaning. And both aspects constitute each other and cannot, therefore, be separated although, as S. Jünger points out correctly, there is a contrast between the semiotic determination of language and the indeterminacy of linguistic meaning attribution. Here, too, the suppositions are strictly system-specific, the presuppositions, however, agent- invariant.

Contrary to the linguistic tradition that distinguishes between the (pre-existing) language-system and the speaker-competence (exploiting this system), the focus in a histories&discourses-oriented view is on communication as a reflexive social process in which the means of communication arise, first of all, through the social qualification of the speakers, and are then differentiated in observation —

one becomes aware that one can speak and one can talk about it. Linguistic elements function as signs *in* communication if and only if they are signs *for* prior communicative co-orientations of speakers and hearers. Linguistic signs synthesise the classes of experiences from which they have emerged. A semiotic relation is not determined by reference or representation but by reflexivity or self-reference in communication. By speaking, or by means of language, we do not (as traditional dualist semiotic concepts suggest) reach out 'into reality' through language but (always) fall back on socially approved uses of signs in communication. Speaking is no be-speaking of intersubjectively pre-established things or events; objects of communication are always objects of *communication*. To paraphrase C. F. von Weizsäcker: Whenever *we* are not communicating about objects, objects are not at stake.

Modelling speaking as a communicative action game, i.e. as a communication action, and modelling language acquisition as the active acquisition of collective knowledge in histories&discourses, indicates that a semiotic model which is fixated on the reference and meaning of signs, overlooks the manifold *conditions* that any form of managing language is subjected to. There is, for instance, the eminent role of *trust* in language acquisition processes as well as in actual communication processes, furthermore the role of *credibility* and the sustained *recognition* of the consequences of previous communications, and finally the importance of the affective involvement and the moral assessment of linguistic operations. In addition to reference and meaning, aspects like function, usage, validity and impact, imputation-imputations and suspected motives, must be adequately taken into account in histories and discourses, and thus we come back again to the fundamental specification of communication as a necessarily reflexive process.

*

The conception of communication developed so far also affects the understanding of *understanding*. Basically, two levels can be distinguished here (with G. Rusch), namely understanding as a cognitive process of meaning construction, and understanding as a social process of the ascription of expectation fulfilment. Both cases have nothing to do with the traditional idea of understanding, i.e. the apprehension of the intended speaker meaning by the hearer, but involve the successful transposition of perceived semiotic materialities into domain-specific processes: one reads a text and starts getting ideas; one observes the linguistic and non-linguistic reactions of communication partners and decides whether they have reacted adequately, i.e. in conformity with one's own expectations, to a communication offer, and so on.

What then is the role played by actual *media offers* in reception? As described above, competent speakers of a natural language know, through years of linguistic socialisation, what expectations are connected with the (largely) socially regulated use of particular communication instruments. They consequently use the process of the sequential perception of the components of media offers to construct cognitive knowledge structures suiting the perceptual context, which result from their interpretation of the materiality of the communication instruments and are inevitably affectively charged and morally assessed in a system-specific way. Thus a linguistic utterance or a media offer does indeed significantly *orient* their perception, without, however, being able to *determine* precisely the system-specific construction of knowledge structures, because all such construction is dependent solely on the states and manners of operation of the system at the time of construction. In other words, meaning constructions are tied to agents but they are not, therefore, necessarily subjective. The consequence is: orientation-orientations always run up against the barriers of necessary system-specificity but they are, therefore, neither arbitrary nor bottomless; for communication operates with the support of two powerful sets of instruments, which functionalise insecurity, i.e. the two frameworks of interactive dependencies, reality model&culture programme and histories&discourses. And that also holds both for the (sense-related) content aspect and the (action-related) relationship aspect of communication.

*

Interactive communication can, however, exploit a second well-known orientation mechanism for the purpose of stabilisation, namely the forms of *non-verbal communication*. This channel permits the encoding primarily of emotional, but also of motivational, moral, and relationship aspects, and is governed by the rule that there can be no non-verbal lie, a rule, however, that knows a substantial number of exceptions. (Top politicians have been trained for a long time now to lie with their bodies just as skilfully as with their mouths.) However, if the suspicion of motive must reasonably be presumed not only with regard to what is said and meant, but also with regard to the manner of the presentation of communication, then it becomes apparent even more drastically that communication must be modelled as a totally and thoroughly reflexive process between communication partners, which includes — from the perception of communication offers to their cognitive reception and life-practical application — exclusively system-specific operations, on the one hand, and feedback loops between the communication partners, on the other. The more unambiguous the express reflexivity of the processes, the higher are the risks of the orientation-orientation, and the more sophisticated will be the preventative measures for securing the success of communications: the moral pressure on the communication partners is increased (commitment to truth, sincerity and authenticity), the density of second-order observation is amplified, the assessment of comprehension results is postponed until the expected connecting operations begin etc. Media societies that have mechanised the use of communicative means in the form of technical and social institutions, exploit the available media systems further for mutual observation, in order to discover and stigmatise unacceptable forms of communication.

*

Apart from the indissoluble connection with cognition, culture and media, there is another relational triple of a special kind for communication, i.e. the relationship with *identity, morality, and truth*. These three topics will be discussed in detail in subsequent chapters; so just a few comments here.

Identity not only has to be created by adequate attributions, it must also be continually presented, and verbal as well as non-verbal means may be employed for that purpose. The blueprints for the presentation of identity are, in the form of communicative schema-knowledge, part of collective knowledge, e.g. relating to the narrative schemas to be used in biographical self-presentations, or the argumentative patterns in the justification of morally problematical actions.

In every communication, with the exception of specific forms of communication like humour, advertising or public relations, the partners tacitly postulate the strict observance of mandatory moral orientation principles like truthfulness, sincerity or reliability, which, in the case of conflict, may even be successfully enforced by law. ('Once a liar, always a liar!', proverbial wisdom warns us.)

And finally, communication functions on the tacit assumption that the knowledge acquired and attributed to others is true; otherwise societies would fall into crises of identity, which would immediately be manifest in crises of communication. — Periods of radical change like the late 18th century in Germany offer a rich variety of relevant illustrative material.

*

In the deliberations so far, actions and communications have been characterised as realisations of culturally programmed schemata whose semantics are communicatively mediated. It seems plausible, therefore, to subsume communication under action, i.e. to conceive of it as a *special form of action*. To all forms of action, as already explained above, two observational perspectives can be applied: processuality and sense orientation (i.e. supposition and presupposition). In order to express this difference as well as its unity terminologically, I suggest an expansion of the concepts of 'communication' as well as the concept of 'action' and to speak of a*ction-communication* and *communication-action*, even though these expressions are anything but elegant. They have been coined to convey that action communicates sense, and that communication is sense-realising action.

Communication-actions as operations cannot be divorced from agents, whereas communication processes as aggregates of communication-actions *can* be characterised/described without paying attention to agents if connections and relations are of primary interest rather than those who supply them. Correspondingly, discourses can also be specified/described as sense-embedding frames for communication processes without paying attention to agents and communication processes, if the primary purpose is the systematisation of communication-actions and communication-processes with regard to theme developments.

Action-communications as operations cannot be divorced from agents either, whereas action sequences as aggregates of action-communications can be characterised/described without paying attention to agents, if the structure and the function of the sequence(s) is the topic of discussion. Correspondingly, histories as sense-oriented syntheses of action sequences can be characterised/described without paying attention to agents and action sequences, if the socially integrating formation of action systems is to be observed.

*

In looking for a category that might serve as the unity of the difference between cognition and communication, we again hit upon the candidate *sense* that was characterised in chapter 3 as the permanent experience of functioning culture programmes or as socially successful difference management. This category is semantically implemented or differentiated through the difference cognition/communication. Both sides of the difference can be observed and described under the double perspective of sense orientation or process. This may yield quite diverse interpretations of 'sense' on either side of the distinction.

In the cognitive domain, sense can be characterised as the *self-orientation competence* of cognitive systems that strives for coherence. Sense emerges from whatever is realised as consistent in the continual process of testing the coherence of the states of a cognitive system. Here again, sense operates as a difference-free category: even intuitively felt sense-deficits are processed by means of semantic differentiations belonging to the category of sense (e.g. senseless, incomprehensible, bottomless etc.).

In the communicative domain, sense can be characterised as the basic mode of the *acceptance or connectibility* of communication offers within the framework of histories&discourses. For this test of acceptance, communication must necessarily fall back on cognitive powers, which again indicates the complementarity of cognition and communication.

'Operation' and 'processuality' in the cognitive domain are characterised as thinking, in the communicative domain as the production, reception and processing of media offers. In both domains, sense is not something given in an other-worldly discourse (according to J. Mitterer), but realises itself as a cognitive and communicative *sense process* in frameworks of histories&discourses.

The consequence of my deliberations is that *society* can be observed under three aspects of diminishing range or dimensionality:

- as the unity of the difference between model of reality and culture programme;
- as the unity of the difference between histories and discourses;

- as the unity of the difference between action-communications and communication-actions.

Such observation may concentrate either on sense orientation or on action-bound processes of 'sense-making', without the possibility, however, of neglecting the other perspective. To emphasise it strongly once more, sense and action as well as systems theories and action theories are not alternative options but complementary *observational variants* that can only be separated from each other analytically. Consequently, all theoretical work should be carried out in full awareness of the requirement of purposive observation management, and not on the basis of some sort of 'theory catholicism'.

8

Process-dependent Realities

If the preceding deliberations are to prove their mettle as an option of non-dualist theory-formation, then it must be demonstrated how the processes in histories&discourses generate, on the operational mode of supposition and presupposition with reference to reality model&culture programme, their *process-dependent realities*; for even according to a non-dualist conception there must be objects and events, observations and descriptions of something etc. To deal with this question, let us first turn to different spheres of objecthood.

*

As already shown in chapter 1, accepting the basic mechanism of supposition and presupposition entails the acceptance of *consciousness* as the instance of reference to something. Consciousness operates in the form of references over and above the auto-constitutive framework of supposition (consciousness of something) and presupposition (without consciousness no something); similarly, the presuppositions of suppositions can only be observed (posited/supposed) as such in reflexive reference — the interplay of supposition and presupposition repeats itself afresh.

As explained in chapter 1, the complementary mechanism of supposition and presupposition must actually be implemented if it is to become effective, i.e. real. Thus the logic of this mechanism entails the assumption that there must be instances which set this mechanism in motion and keep it in motion (as is happening in the argument presented here), i.e. it entails the assumption of *agents*.

Let us continue with the problem of *objects* in the broadest sense. As expounded above, we can deal with objects only as referents or as products of reference. Objects *for us exist* only by virtue of such reference — from acts of consciousness to communications — , and they can, therefore, be specified only as system-specific realities, however we choose to formulate such specifications. All our acts of reference *posit something as something* specified in some way, they constitute objecthoods of whatever kind by applying the difference self-reference/other-reference; and they must, in fact, apply this difference so as to be capable of realising themselves as the concrete chosen references and nothing else, i.e. posit themselves. And this supposition necessarily operates over and above a set of presuppositions specific for an active system. Without the constitution of objects, consciousness is inconceivable, and without consciousness, objecthood. Both are strictly complementary.

This endorses the insight of constructivist observation theories that have modelled objecthood as the result of observation/observer-processes. The difference to the present approach is that previous constructivist observation theories have called the observer a *constructor* of objects, which unavoidably begged the question as to whether the construction was a physical or just a semantic one. In the deliberations presented here, the topic of construction is not dealt with at all because their intention is neither to assert nor to deny existence or reality but to establish conclusively that it only makes sense to speak of objects if there is a relation between a consciousness, i.e. an observer, and an object of consciousness or an observation result. As soon as there is, it can be experienced and described as a unity of the difference between consciousness and object of consciousness, of self- and other-reference; and both in the experiences and the descriptions *objects* may be quite meaningfully discussed. One must always be very careful, however, not to separate the object tacitly from the complementary relationship between consciousness and object, and to treat it 'as such '.

*

Similar conditions obtain for the constitution of *space* and *time* through processes of consciousness or conscious reference.

Every supposition as the realisation of a distinction necessarily posits space and time because the transition from a presupposition to a supposition realises itself as an operation that can only be envisaged in space and time. The processuality and relationality of our conscious processes thus inevitably generates space and time. 'Time is an effect of the mode of operation of consciousness; consciousness generates time because it can only operate in time. […] Time is a product of consciousness…' (O. Jahraus 2001:74). The same holds for space as the unity of temporal difference.

The modalities of space and time determine everything that we can experience in histories&discourses and whatever we can say about histories and discourses, because they allow us to mark the coordinates of transitions. As already said: *everything* continues without interruption. Every activity of consciousness, every communication, every action builds on the foregoing and carries it further; there is no temporal gap in processes or in observations and descriptions. Whereas we can give the past and the future an infinite extension, in principle, the present is an extension-free limiting value between before and after, or — in phenomenological parlance — an itinerant horizon. 'Always is Now', the Viennese artist A. Glück once said. Everything that happens at all, happens right here and now. Whatever happens, happens necessarily in the presence of observers; and everything that happens in their world, happens at the same time. The Church Father St. Augustine coined the memorable formula: '... there are three times, the present of the past, the present of the present, and the present of the future.' Everything depends on how we interrupt this flow, these unending transitions, this *all-inclusive nowness* (M. McLuhan), how we discontinue it through suitable processes, so that structures may emerge that, by supplying discontinuity, allow us the observation of temporal dynamics, in the first place. Time, more precisely: temporality, helps us with this operation. It allows us to interrupt the flow of processes and to occupy ourselves with something specific and nothing else. In our actions and communications we posit time by presupposing differences: action/non-action, before/after, now/later. On the one hand, time indicates the time-consuming aspect of actions and processes of any kind, on the other hand, it allows for the formation of structures by transforming experiences into solid expectations. (N. Luhmann speaks of the irritability of the present by the future; we could also speak of the irritability of the present by the past.) And it is only through the reflexive dovetailing of perception, repetition and time, one may conclude, that cognitive and communicative realities arise.

Space and time can only be observed through reciprocal observation. Space can be observed through the unity of temporal difference, spatial unity through temporal difference. Time can be observed through the unity of spatial difference, temporal difference through spatial unity. The present can only be imagined and experienced as temporal *and* spatial presence. Spatiality and temporality are irreducible in principle but remain hidden from us as the fundamental instruments of our 'reality construction'.

The present, and this involves equally present actuality (how else could we experience the present), we can conclude from these deliberations, can be modelled theoretically as the unity of the difference between space and time. We live in frameworks of action and communication, in histories and discourses, which allow us orientation both through their inner logic and through the orientation by the framework of interactive dependencies reality model&culture programme. Semantically implemented and affectively charged conceptions of space and time apparently only emerge in our culturally programmed histories and discourses, and our talk about space and time is oriented towards histories and discourses that admit of the rule-bound and socially successful transition of states into states.

*

As already repeatedly stressed, everything that happens takes place in *transitions*, in the Between, in the While, i.e. in the form of spatial temporality or temporal spatiality. For us, there are no definite beginnings and endings (not least because we can experience neither our birth nor our death consciously), but only transitions. Transitions appear in histories and discourses in the form of connecting operations; things proceed in meaningful ways, we feel and assert causality. Time is tied to the concomitant experience of the here-and-now in histories and discourses that serve as the system of coordinates for all experiences and descriptions. Time exists because we produce histories and discourses — not vice versa; such a constellation we could neither perceive nor describe.

Transitions are imagined differences, which change into lived distinctions that in turn revert into differences again. Always is now, because we possess the concepts 'always' and 'now'; and we always use them now in order to discontinue time by means of the present. We therefore hit upon the paradox that time is, on the one hand, the decisive category for all processualisation, but that time itself is, on the other hand, only observable and describable as a function of processes of consciousness, experience and description in histories and discourses. And this is why we find it so difficult to abandon the deeply rooted conviction that time is independent of us and pre-exists our actions in histories and discourses, that it flows according to its own laws, as it were, through our histories and discourses.

Transitions constitute themselves precisely in what they are not, namely in every new system state, although they are nothing else but uninterrupted transformations of states. But transitions keep the onset, the transition, and the arrival in the transition from experience to description, en bloc at the ready, as it were, because we delay our describing, we search for discontinuities, we want to apprehend and specify something clearly as something. This means that transitions are only identifiable as unities of distinctions for as long as we apply the proper semantic differentiations. Transitions are the mode of the emergence of reality that always appears to us in the present because consciousness, due to its directedness, prefers to describe itself in the mode of presence. The reality of transition is the transition of reality into realities. This is why reality and present can only be imagined as complementaries.

This complementarity is further expressed by the fact that *sense* and time must be envisaged as indissolubly linked. Sense relationships are time relationships, and vice versa. Sense relationships only *make* sense if they orient operations, if they permit the prescription of what makes sense before, after, with, and for, each other. Time relationships are meaningfully specifiable only as sense relationships, i.e. as temporal forms of sense. The temporal form of sense and the sense form of time allow us to forget in our histories and discourses that we can leave the flow of processes only with the help of references to the ordering categories of sense and time.

If we describe time as an independent social dimension of sense condensed from actions, in which we experience and interpret our linguistic and non-linguistic actions in histories and discourses, then action as a basic social event is, as it were, a sort of embodiment of time in the sense that time can be co-experienced through the realisation of the body. Time unites past, present, and future in the compact sense structures, into which actions in histories and discourses are transformed. Everything that happens, happens in histories in the present. Everything we know, we know from the past. Everything we do, we do for the future. Consequently, the sense form of time transforms events and happenings from points in time into *histories* and *discourses*.

Time is experienced through *differences*, e.g. through the difference between pre-histories and post-histories, between now and soon, between news and repetition. All these differences are in turn specified temporally, as transitions, as contradiction or corroboration. It must be taken into account, however, that in the observation of time, the time of observation and the time observed are not identical.

We employ the differences of histories and discourses as indicators of the passing of time. In histories and discourses there is, therefore, no alternative to time. There is no imaginable alternative to space and time, because consciousness as a process both constitutes, and by virtue of its processing simultaneously uses, time and space.

*

As already expounded several times, *schemata* of various kinds play an important role in all kinds of action. Schemata that speed up cognitive and communicative processes by turning them into routines, may also be described as *condensations of time*. Once stabilised, they take care of the provision of time budgets, as it were, which can be used for purposes other than the termination of elementary cognitive and communicative operations, e.g. for differentiations, complex evaluations, or extended comparisons. (We can see at one glance that we are standing in front of a deciduous tree, and can then immediately tackle the question as to whether the tree is a beech or an oak, whether we want to trim or fell it etc.)

Temporal categories and schemata have, due to the histories-and-discourses-shape of human life, always served as ordering schemata for experiences as well as for memories and narrations, not least for the reason that temporal and spatial relations are closely linked with ideas of cause and effect. If everything that happens, happens simultaneously, then we need efficient *process interrupters*.

The past then assumes the form of experience and memory, the present the form of event and experience, the future the form of expectation and design. The past 'belongs' to me, whenever experiences made in the past can be applied in the present or emerge as narratives suitable for the production of memories. The future 'belongs' to me, whenever it triggers action in the present. The present 'belongs' to me as long as I am conscious.

*

Our references are not only directed at the treatment of the difference self/something as an object but also at the difference *ego/alter* as interaction partners (see chapter 11). This difference necessarily results from the reflexivity of perception. A and B perceive each other, and they are able to perceive that each of them is perceived by the other. Knowledge results (A knows that B knows), which may in turn become reflexive (A knows that B knows that A knows). A and B thus live in a partially shared history, in which, through the mechanism of reflexivity, expectations are built up with regard to the expectations of the other. These expectation-expectations provide the opportunity of social, i.e. other-related, action and thus basically also communication, as K. Merten (1977) has shown in detail. A and B must now, with every supposition that is relevant to the other, implicitly presuppose that the other mobilises a similar mechanism of supposition and presupposition. Consequently, both partners acquire the right, despite the simultaneous constitution of double contingency (in the understanding of T. Parsons and N. Luhmann), to generalise their own cognitive operations as community- or society-specific. In other words: action and communication succeed solely on the basis of the operative fiction that some collective knowledge with regard to the semantics of suppositions and presuppositions is assumed to be generally prescribed in the given community/society. The obligatory orientation towards this operative fiction decides about the inclusion into the particular community/society, which is constituted and preserved by the difference we/the others. In other words, the difference alter/ego is enforced per reflexivity by the requirement that socially relevant perceptions have to be confirmed by others.

*

How can the genesis of the operative fiction of collective knowledge, which has so often been invoked by now, be specified more precisely? My hypothesis is that *knowledge* can be specified as schematised and condensed experience which has been gained from action and communication and has proved its action-relevant mettle. In order to be effective, knowledge must (potentially) be incessantly generated cognitively (e.g. by way of active thought or recall) and represented communicatively. In order to become socially relevant, knowledge needs internal order as well as a perceptible materiality so as to allow for reflexive reference.

Internal order arises through the development of a socially binding framework of interactive dependencies reality model&culture programme from the genesis of categories and their operative provision by means of semantic differentiations, relations and evaluations. Categories and semantic differentiations may again be specified as schematisations that can be used for the orientation of experiences.

Knowledge acquires a *perceptible materiality* as soon as its internal structures manifest themselves in reliable semiotic figures of expression that render knowledge communicable. Such figures of expression arise with natural *languages*, which communicatively stabilise models of reality and allow for the reflexive handling of the references to such models of reality in the knowledge mode: one can say what one knows, because one knows that others can know what one says and how one says it. Languages, with their differential signifying structure, materialise the distinction systems of the underlying model of reality which they, at the same time, concretise semiotically and semantically. Languages thus provide the conditions for creating models of reality via culture programmes in histories and discourses agent-relevant as communication-actions and action-communications.

*

This concludes the short survey of the genesis of process-dependent realities 'from the spirit' of reflexive reference and their schematisation. The overall aim has been to show that despite the great variability of spheres like consciousness, agents, space and time, object and event, schema and sense, knowledge and language, or alter and ego, no ontological assertions of existence are required to reveal the corresponding realities. It is, in fact, sufficient to describe the reality-constituting status of the generative processes resulting from concrete references. A concise formulation characterising this strategy may be derived from the fundamental insight supplied by J. Mitterer: the description of the object and the object of the description must be viewed as being identical.

9
Beyond Dualism

The reflections carried out so far have clearly been governed by the inclination to avoid any realist ontological assertions, and to describe objects of any kind as components or as results of *processes*. This inclination derives from the kind of non-dualist philosophical approaches that have been developed during the last few years, first and foremost by J. Mitterer. My own position in the context of these approaches will be briefly outlined in what follows.

*

The mainstream of European philosophy and science has undoubtedly been moulded by fundamentally dualist convictions. It has been stated often enough that this is the reason why the problems of this philosophical tradition with regard to reality and knowledge, statement and truth, action and value, language and reference etc. are irresolvable in principle. They are irresolvable in principle because they all operate with a *petitio principii*. Once the components of a complementary framework have been separated from each other and declared independent ontic entities, there is no longer any possibility of reconstructing the processuality and reflexivity of the complementary framework, and one finally runs aground on the argumentative 'riff' that without consciousness (reference) and description (interruption) nothing 'exists' that could be reflected and described.

As long as the dualist paradigm remains in force, there is no other option than a realist or idealist theory of knowledge (of whatever make-up). In order to make progress with regard to the problems mentioned, a non-dualist approach must be worked out. This will be attempted here. And the attempt will begin with a determined re-positioning of the point of departure of the argument, i.e. the starting point of the discourse. A few comments.

*

Dualist theorists usually begin with assumptions of existence, and primarily with the assumption of the existence of subjects and objects — for instance, with the notorious table of the philosopher, which allegedly exists as such and can therefore be regarded as an entity independent of the observer. In making these unquestioned assumptions, one has immediately traded in all the well-known grand philosophical problems like reality, knowledge, truth etc., because this dualist starting operation dishonestly suppresses the fact that assertions of existence no less than denials of existence cannot but be made by agents in concrete communication contexts — where else. We assert or deny *in a particular communication situation in a particular way and manner* that there is a table before us, that reality exists or not, that we are capable of discovering the laws of nature or not. C. F. von Weizsäcker has found the following succinct formula for this insight: 'Whenever we speak seriously of reality, *we* speak of reality, if nobody speaks of reality, reality is not at stake.' (1980:142)

Here the problem of reality is prudently *dis*solved by neither asserting nor denying the existence of a reality, and by stating, at the same time, that only in concrete references something like a real thing may play a role as the relatum or referent of a conscious act of reference. Assertions and denials of existence are, therefore, useless starting strategies because they — like the notorious question of 'the reality' — answer themselves paradoxically: the question of reality one can only pose in a reality that is consequently 'set in being as reality'. Or in a formulation by S. Jünger: Reality is determined by the efficacy of references. (2002:58) The assertion 'X exists', strictly speaking, states nothing but 'X is the result of a distinction'.

The trouble with dualist theories of knowledge can be avoided from the start if one does not begin with objects and subjects and the quality of the relations between them, but with processes. 'Perceive', 'observe' or 'describe' are transitive verbs that describe actions, which can simply by way of a change of observational perspective be (analytically) divided up into action-carrier/agent, action realisation, and action result. A perception is necessarily the perception of an agent who, in a concrete situation, perceives something as something. In this process, no single component can be dispensed with without dissolving the complex as a whole. Something *is for us* always and necessarily *something* seen, described, imagined, made, carried etc. *as something,* although we can postulate it in discourse as an object divorced from such concrete actions. And in such frameworks of action, the question of reality does not arise simply because nobody could sensibly pose it. How could I possibly, when perceiving something, question *whether* I am perceiving something? (Naturally, I can ask myself *what* I am perceiving here and now.) The object of the description and the description of the object merge, as J. Mitterer has argued often enough. In perception, none of us can, therefore, retreat behind perception, in order to compare what is perceived with what is not yet perceived, for the purpose of checking the objectivity of perception, as Democritus seems to have pointed out already. Wherever something emerges 'as an object' or as whatever else, it emerges, as it were, on the umbilical cord of a process — *as* something perceived, imagined, made, or described. Whereas dualists have to assume that the table is already there before I can perceive it and continues to exist as a table even if I do not perceive it, non-dualists dissolve these assumptions by speaking exclusively of perceived, imagined, made, cleaned, or laid tables. The reality of the table is, to enlist S. Jünger's help once again, determined by the efficacy of references. And references need points of reference that, through their differentiation, become observable as references, in the first place; they need — to put it differently — the difference self-reference/other-reference (*I direct my* attention at *something*, *I speak* about *something*). This cognitive manoeuvre produces — as shown above — its own *process-specific reality* without having to postulate process-independent ontological objects. In such a non-dualist position, objects can be designed as quasi concomitant results of processes — the question of their reality remaining implausible if and as long as object and reference are to be taken as strictly complementary.

Now, since we can envisage references, as already stated, only in a strictly system-specific way, the objects 'are' equally system-specific. The question as to whether we can overcome this system-specificity by means of suitable cognitive manoeuvres and apprehend reality in itself (as is postulated by approximation theories of truth), eliminates itself in this train of argument as an unanswerable question

—with all due consequences for theories of truth (see chapter 13).

It may now be objected that the claim to non-dualism of the theory presented here is illusory inasmuch as it is constantly dealing with differences and distinctions, which are the very principle of the construction of all realities. This objection can be invalidated in the following way.

It is correct that the argument developed so far insisted that we can only imagine, perceive or describe something as something within the framework of the processes of the semantic differentiation of categories and the asymmetric division of semantic differentiations into distinctions. Only by making use of differences, the construction of identity as a unity of difference becomes possible, and this also obtains for observations of the second order that operate with their own sets of differences.

Such *process-bound difference management* must not, however, be confused with a dualist ontological division of the world into spheres of subjects and objects, i.e. with an argument that interprets the strictly process-bound use of differentiations and distinctions ontologically by separating process and process result on an essentialist basis (and not only by observational analysis), thereby creating the problem of their potential relations. The problem is not the reference to something by way of difference-positing in object-constitutive processes, but its dualistic re-interpretation that must be dissolved by the theory of difference in order to evade epistemological dualism.

10
Interim Summary 2

The aim of the reflections carried out so far was to show that, and how, working with elementary categories allows for the derivation of objects and structures of our histories&discourses-reality without recourse to an external ontology. The experiences resulting from this working method are the subject of this brief interim summary.

The decision to take the logically auto-constitutive framework of supposition and presupposition as the starting point has led to two insights:

- It is implausible to postulate a presupposition-free beginning for anything whatsoever, not even for a theory, because every action and every communication is necessarily tied into preceding and ongoing histories and discourses.
- Every supposition is selective and contingent because, basically, another option could always have been chosen.

If suppositions are considered to be processual uses of presuppositions that realise themselves in suppositions, and if consciousness is defined as reference that can attain self-awareness only through reflexivity, then the necessity of consciousness and suppositions constitutes space and time as well as objects in space and time.

Reflexive perception generates knowledge that is ascribed to others and, as an operative fiction (collective expectation of collective expectations), permits socialisation. On this basis, communication and language can arise and be used effectively, although each of the communicating systems can only operate with the help of its system-specific difference management. Collective ascribed knowledge requires internal order and concrete possibilities of observation. Such order is guaranteed by the evolution of categories and semantic differentiations in the shape of a model of reality in which experiences concerned with problem-solving are schematised in a socially relevant (i.e. viable) way.

These patterns of knowledge are endowed with a communicatively manageable and observable semiotic materiality due to the semiotic expression capabilities of language, in which societal experiences are sedimented, as it were, in the shape of collective knowledge. This collective knowledge can then be 'built into' the individual production of knowledge in socialisation processes and, consequently, furnish agents with the competence for the production and application of such allegedly collective knowledge.

Schematisations also shape the areas of action and communication in histories&discourses in that schemata permit the meaningful synthesis of singular events to actions of particular types, and thus help to render both the performance and the interpretation of actions socially connectible. Actions as suppositions orient themselves meaningfully by means of action schemata as socially valid presuppositions. Thus the observational variance practised so far opens up the vista for the complementary double aspect of all action and communication, namely sense orientation and process orientation.

Interim Summary 2

In all these considerations, the system-dependence of all suppositions (the 'cognitive autonomy' of agents) must adequately be taken into account because it excludes any direct intervention in operating systems. Thus reflexivity as a fundamental mechanism re-enters the stage. For if the supposition of distinctions within the space of presuppositions unfolded by categories and semantic differentiations marks the path of our orientations in histories and discourses, i.e. the sequence of meaningful actions that comprises our human existence, then it follows that we orient ourselves by our own orientations, wherever we believe these orientations to have come from. The resulting guideline is: change to reflexive forms, e.g. from learning to self-learning, from observation to self-observation, from linear intervention to orientation to self-orientation in processes of teaching and learning, from mutual understanding to orientation-orientation that is confirmed by expected follow-up actions or follow-up communications, and not by the mutual matching of cognitive operations between the orientation partners; — we intuitively assume that communication is accompanied by thinking, but no doubt mainly for narcissistic reasons.

The reasons for this turnaround manoeuvre are only too apparent: cognitive systems must encode all the events in their environment in such a way as to make them accessible to system-specific treatment/processing, and such treatment/processing together with the evaluation of the results is performed exclusively by the management of the orientation apparatus under system control (= complexity building). This makes clear that the environment of a system comprises exactly those environmental relations and environmental contacts of the system, which enable the system to handle the difference self-reference/other-reference.

Correspondingly, the interaction and communication of cognitive systems is subject to the ever-present constraints of selection-dependent contingency, and systems and their environments obviously constitute each other.

*

With the fundamental development of all cognitive and socially central types of processes towards reflexivity, important guidelines have been laid down for all subsequent theory formation in the sense that particular options are no longer admissible (however respectable they may appear in the annals of science). This concerns particularly input/output-models, exchange models, procedures of control and prediction, or models of representation and approximation. They are replaced by model types like self-organisation and construction, reflexivity, orientation-orientation and selection simulation, viability and regress interruption, which are mostly discussed in contemporary discourse under headings such as systems theory and constructivism.

The basic idea is always the same: if observing systems can only observe what they observe and how they observe (this is why it makes no sense to want to ask or state what pre-exists observation or what the observed is in itself), then the direction of the observation must run from the system to the environment and not vice versa; for then the observing system constructs its own states of order as well as a/its environment, through the recursiveness of its own operations (i.e. through cognitive reflexivity). Certainly not by fabricating environments ex nihilo (for without environment no creation of cognitive order), but by developing an internal representation for realities/environments through its own operations and perceived environmental factors, which can then be tested for its viability in actions and communications. In other words: the relationship between system and environment is complementary, too, and operates on the basis of the mechanism of supposition and presupposition; for if environment is specified as the set of the environmental relations of a system, then system and environment are of equal importance, as it were, although the direction of observation always originates in the system.

Now, to avoid any paleo-constructivist subject-fixation, we must insist on the kind of contextualisation which has been sketched out in the histories&discourses-philosophy in the form of the argument that, although all operations are definitely system-bound, a clear distinction must be made between operation or process, and sense orientation, as the components of an auto-constitutive framework. Without the embedding of the framework of interactive dependencies of histories&discourses into the framework of interactive dependencies of reality model&culture programme, in which all agents are enmeshed, social action would be impossible.

However, the 'commandment of reflexivity' also obtains for this complex interdependence between operation and sense orientation. This means that the orientation potentials in the quoted frameworks of interactive dependencies reach far beyond the single individual with the range and the obligations they can claim, and this is why they qualify at all as suitable for the social, and the system integration, of agents; but if these orientation potentials are not used by agents for their (however consciously enacted) *self-orientation*, they remain without function. *Sense is not given, it must be made.* On the other hand, there is no chance either not really 'to make sense' in every supposition, because sense is simply always presupposed — we cannot realise a presupposition-free supposition.

*

For these reasons, however, all operations of agents are fraught with twofold *insecurity*: What orientation potentials are actually executed in histories&discourses? And how does this execution manifest itself in detail? As such executions, as a rule, cannot or need not be controlled by consciousness, both their re-enactment and their control is difficult, as everyone knows who has attempted to understand other people's actions. And an attempt of a communicative thematisation may prove to be no less problematical, because it must necessarily be realised within the framework of the orientation potentials for linguistic and non-linguistic actions in histories&discourses. This becomes especially clear in the application of orientation-orientation in the affective sphere. — For this very reason novels and films have been untiring in trying to present examples of what one must do to be loved if/because one is in love oneself.

Consciousness, communication and non-linguistic action always integrate two directions of orientation: self- and other-orientation. Agents orient themselves towards a particular (expected) goal; at the same time, however, such orientations are (intentionally or not) supplied to other agents as orientation-orientations, i.e. as options for self-orientation.

Orientation-orientation as the instantiation of *reflexivity* makes clear, and without recourse to biology, what can be understood by operative closure. If a cognitive system cannot objectively refer to an existing real environment, if, therefore, every environment contact realises itself as a peculiar form of self-contact that is subjected to the special semantics of an object world, then the manoeuvres of self-orientation of this system can be specified as follows: perceptions are measured by perceptions, experiences are checked by experiences and expectations (as condensed experiences), knowledge gleaned from actions and communications is processed by knowledge. Reality appears in these operations as an experience of success, so to speak (reality as an emergent phenomenon), and thus as unquestionably real as it appears to agents in histories&discourses. Realities, one could say, are only then lived by us and successfully lived, when the conditions of this living experience have been rendered invisible.

*

In order for orientation-orientations to stand a chance of success at all, important presuppositions must be fulfilled, first and foremost the operative fictions as shared collective knowledge, and the enmeshing of the participants in actions and communications in histories and discourses.

Whereas these presuppositions are effective in the agents as implicit and, as a rule, unconscious parameters of control and transform their individual praxis into social praxis, societies have developed yet other possibilities of control, which mainly function consciously. These instances of control can be assigned to three types: hierarchical ones (religion, law), heterarchical ones (common monitoring of all kinds, money, markets of all kinds), and schematic ones (patterns of conformity, *habitus* according to P. Bourdieu, institutionalisations of any kind). They are effective both on local and global levels. The degree of success of orientation-orientations is high with social groups that intensively discuss common interests and values (as e.g. with citizens' initiatives, Greenpeace etc.). It falls demonstrably in cases of conflict, in which everyone insists on the truth of their own orientation.

Orientation-orientation is a useful formula for solving the problem of how to deal with the difference between cognitive autonomy and social control. Whereas the concept of structural coupling, which is often employed for the solution of this problem, always implies some sort of direct connection, orientation-orientation indicates that cognitive autonomy and social orientation are not only equally possible but also mutually constitutive, because the operative fictions used for orientation-orientation can be both cognitively processed and communicatively thematised and justified.

*

In the preceding deliberations the mechanism of *reflexivity* has proved to be a highly generative mechanism that more or less generates its own processual ontology. It begins with consciousness, which in reflexive reference to itself becomes conscious of itself. But it is also evident in the production of a socially viable order in other central domains of histories and discourses. This process will be elucidated in the following with regard to the relational triple that was identified as specific to communication in chapter 7, namely *identity*, *morality*, and *truth*.

The basic idea is always the same: individuals like societies present themselves to other individuals and societies in the mode of the difference alter/ego or we/the others. This presentation is subject to two conditions: it must be coherent for the presenter, and it must be accepted and quasi reflected back by the others. To meet both conditions, individuals just like societies need *identity regulations* to make sure that these precarious processes of attribution do not go astray.

The situation is similar for the regulation of the interactions between agents with regard to value orientation, and for the regulation of communications in discourses with regard to truth. In both cases, strategies of cultural contingency treatment as well as — imposed by these — interruption mechanisms for infinite regresses are required. These tasks are accomplished by morality as a legitimation interrupter and truth as an argument/justification interrupter.

11
Identity

As was already explained in the interim summary 2, identity belongs to those products of reflexivity, which aid societies in dealing with two centrally important differences, namely the difference alter/ego and the difference we/the others. The mechanism of supposition and presupposition, fundamental to this treatment, may be outlined as follows.

*

Ego *posits* itself by reference to itself *as ego* against the foil of the *presupposition* that there is another ego apart from itself, i.e. alter, that in turn posits ego as the presupposition of its own ego-supposition. Without the possibility of this difference-supposition and difference-exploitation, every supposition of ego as ego would be pointless and without function. At the same time, we realise that, with consciousness as the reflexive reference, the *self* is necessarily supposed *qua* self-consciousness. The self is the point of departure for all references of consciousness and the domain of reference for the self-ascription of intentions, action capability, will etc.

We are thus faced with a double supposition. Consciousness posits itself in the course of its reflexive reference to itself as self, 'self' meaning nothing but the direction of reference. 'Self' is, consequently, a synonym for 'self-consciousness' and functions—as G. Roth (2001:326) has argued in great detail—as the centre of a virtual world that we experience as our experiential world or actuality.

The *cognitive self* posits itself as a *social ego* through the difference-supposition to (another ego as) alter. This process rests on the reflexivity of perception. A and B perceive each other and are able to perceive that this perception is reciprocal. The result is a particular kind of knowledge (A knows that B knows), which may in turn become reflexive: A knows that B knows that A knows, and they both know that they *ascribe* this knowledge to themselves and to each other.

The following aspects of this constellation of reflexivity are of particular importance:

- The difference between ego and alter produces itself, because neither side could constitute itself separately as part of this difference.

- The constitution of this difference is dependent on ascription and voluntary affirmation by alter, i.e. it functions as a social process. As socially relevant actions have to be affirmed by others, action dictates the difference-supposition alter/ego.

- Through the mutual ascription of difference-knowledge, ego and alter constitute a partially shared history that co-orients their interactions.

- Cognitive self-identity as an order of reference of consciousness, and social identity as the mutually constitutive management of the difference ego/alter, depend on each other in the mode of supposition and presupposition—without self-identity social identity would be bottomless, without the possibility of social identity self-identity would have no function.

This hypothesis concerning the genesis and the function of identity may be summed up as follows: consciousness attains consciousness of itself by realising that it is consciousness of something. This cognitive identity of consciousness may be termed 'self'. Cognitive identity experiences itself as specific cognitive identity by realising that there are other cognitive identities with which it is not identical. This social identity of the self may be termed 'ego'. In both cases identity emerges as the result of a process deriving from constellations of reflexivity.

Cognitive and social identity once conscious will remain unchanged until a new presentation or legitimation is required. On such occasions, identity functions as a kind of knowledge about how reference to self can or ought to be enacted.

The function of identity may be specified as the development and stabilisation of references that the self attributes to itself, thus performing the meta-stable transition syntheses. In this respect, identity is, as S. Jünger puts it, continuity of change as change of continuity.

*

Strictly speaking, however, the difference alter/ego must be differentiated once more. 'Ego' stands for the self-image and the self-description worked out by a cognitive system of and for itself, ' alter' for a partner image formed by ego of an agent perceived in the environment. The same distinction is made by alter who designs himself as ego and the other as alter in his environment. Thus we have two versions of ego and alter, each bound to another self as the point of reference or point of origin of observations. The observing self can now observe this difference by way of self-observations and achieve self-consciousness through the simulation of other-observation. Ego thus uses the operations of alter (i.e. a perceived environmental phenomenon) for the constitution of self-consciousness. In other words, it produces the unstable state of order 'self-consciousness' without an external manager, i.e. by self-organisation, and this production of order is materialised, as it were, by ego narrating himself as the coherent sense of his histories — and there ego cannot err.

Put differently: self-observation and other-observation of both cognitive self-identity and social ego-identity stand in a multiply reflexive relationship with each other, which demands constant interpretation and is correspondingly highly hazardous and contingent. The observation conditions constituted in this way operate against the backdrop of what is *unobservable* in these processes, namely the other-observation of one's own identity. Therefore our self, as experience teaches us, remains 'forever alone' in all social interactions.

*

The derivation of identity from the fluctuating interplay of suppositions and presuppositions, of references and attributions, entails the conclusion that identity is not a solid given, but can only be seen as a process and its results. Identity must always be created anew by drawing structures, in the shape of self-descriptions, from the permanent transitions of cognitive as well as social processes through reflexive interruption (discontinuation), or by imposing such structures. Identity production necessarily occurs in histories and discourses, and it consequently participates, consciously or unconsciously, in the patterns of order available to agents in a society in the form of the frameworks of interactive dependencies of histories&discourses as well as reality model&culture programme. Observed self-references thus realise themselves as cognitive self-descriptions (self-communications), automatically employing socially available patterns of narration and argumentation.

Identity results, according to the preceding reflections, from observed self-references in self-descriptions (identity-formation for oneself) and self-representations (identity-formation for others). Both processes take place in concrete relational spaces, i.e. in histories and discourses.

*

In the *representation* of social identity it is of decisive importance to maintain the continuity of representation for the relevant groups of reference, and to make sure that the representational variants in different groups not only remain compatible for the representing agent but are accepted or at least tolerated by the group members. If, however, ambiguities and conflicts arise, then so-called negative identity or pathological reactions in the form of psychoses or neuroses may develop.

The communicative self-descriptions in which identity representations are realised, must make use of socially acceptable meaning schemata, mainly in the form of narrative schemata that agents mutually attribute to each other as collective knowledge. On this basis, such representations can be expected to be understood and to release desirable follow-up operations.

In cognitive as well as communicative self-descriptions — prototypically in autobiographies — we, as agents, devise a dynamic biographical order to which we adjust our actions and communications in histories and discourses. We orient our self-descriptions as well as our self-representations by the observed other-observations and other-descriptions fabricated and communicated by others. That we are forced to 'read' such descriptions in order to understand them, once more indicates the high contingency of all identity-relevant processes. In brief: the formation and stabilisation of identity depends on whether agents succeed in synthesising events into meaningful actions, and actions into meaningful histories, and in self-attributing them.

*

Cognitive self-descriptions as well as communicative self-representations do not occur continuously but require *occasions* that are deemed relevant. Such occasions present themselves in the cognitive sphere whenever gaps, incoherencies or contradictions are noticed in self-descriptions. In the communicative sphere this happens whenever others direct our attention to gaps, incoherencies or contradictions in our self-representation, or even call it in question.

Processes of identity formation acquire their *specificity* from the selectivity of the histories and the participation of agents in discourses as well as from agents' imagination and creativity. Of relevance here is the recognisability and the assessment of the difference between one's own and other histories (i.e. something that might be called the ordinariness or extraordinariness of a 'life'), the kind and weight of the discourses in which agents participate, and finally the contributions they make. It is no accident, therefore, that extraordinary contributions like theories or inventions are branded with the names of the originators and thus become permanent parts of their biographies.

The degree of public familiarity and social or political influence of particular identity-representations is certainly decisive for the degree of their power to secure general *acceptance*. Whereas in earlier centuries the powerful were in a position to dictate both the kind and the acceptance of their self-representation, these possibilities have become rather scarce in modern media-culture societies. The main goal now is primarily to maintain the coherence of self-representation in sufficient measure despite the continual observation by 'the media'.

In this situation another important aspect of identity-formation becomes apparent, and that is the aspect of the *memory-dependence* of identity (autobiographical memory). The implicit promise carried by an identity-representation: 'I am myself and I shall remain myself both for myself and for you' can only be kept if the problem-solving memory of an agent functions both for purposes of foresight and hindsight. Only then the presupposition of the self-representation of agents becomes credible, namely, that they are in control of the coherence and plausibility of their histories and discourses (i.e. rulers of their own houses), their past (i.e. their recollections) and their future (i.e. their plans). The order and sense achieved *qua* identity cannot be related to the currently given histories and discourses but must constitute arrangements of broader range, as it were. One must be able to recall all the relevant self-related narrations that one has presented to others in different constellations and situations as 'this is me '. One must also be able to recall all the self-descriptions that one has fabricated in the course of time in order to be able to experience them as coherent and continuous. And the main point here is not, as with recall in general, whether the recollections are objectively true but solely whether they can *effectively* create coherence and legitimation.

*

Processes of identity-formation and identity-representation may be observed with regard to cognitive, affective, and moral aspects, all closely inter-connected.

- The cognitive aspect first and foremost concerns truth and sincerity. If we want to be judged positively by others, then our self-representations must meet the societal expectations of sincerity and truthfulness. — It is not without good reason that novels and plays abound with debates of the theme 'living a lie'.
- The affective aspect concerns the problem that identity-production and identity-representation are felt to be satisfactory only if a positive equilibration of pleasure and pain (in the sense of L. Ciompi) can be achieved through a balancing of personal desires and needs with societal demands.
- The moral aspect deals with the need to have a 'clear conscience' with regard to values, i.e. not to feel condemned to play the hypocrite. Furthermore, we must present ourselves as morally sound to our interaction partners in order to win their approval. For such reasons, moral criticism hits us particularly hard because it can decisively weaken our social reputation. This is demonstrated most tangibly, for instance, in political debates when factual arguments peter out or matter no longer, and the antagonists are suspected or even accused of a lack of moral integrity.

*

Let us turn to the difference we/the others, i.e. the question of *social identity*. Many of the arguments introduced so far can be employed for the clarification of this question, in particular the general assumption that identity is a product of reflexivity.

Identity

In parallel to the distinction between cognitive and social identity for agents, a distinction between cognitive and communicative aspects may also be drawn with regard to 'society' (understood as a fiction of discourse). There the cognitive aspect is specified by the framework of interactive dependencies reality model&culture programme that must naturally be available if a social identity in the form of the handling of the distinction we/the others is to be based on this presupposition. This difference must be accepted and socially attributed by the members of the society as well as by other societies.

The difference we/the others is built up chiefly through narrative strategies of self-assurance and historiography in a process of constructing a sort of social autobiography of a society (as understood by A. and J. Assmann). This social autobiography is, on the one hand, distributed across the cognitive domains of all society-members, it is, on the other hand, incorporated in the organisations of a society.

Difference-forming narration, distinguishing between what is proper to oneself and what is foreign, operates mainly with two strategies, i.e. with *memory politics* and with *stereotyping*.

- Memory politics is performed by 'adjusting' the past of a society communicatively in such a way as to make it an agent of contemporary self-consciousness. Beautification, omission and suppression serve here as suitable procedures in dealing with archives that are thus used selectively according to interest and motive – the more comprehensive the archives, the greater the selectivity.

- Stereotyping serves the creation of easily surveyable and narratively conveyable complexity in the description and evaluation of 'the others'. It reduces communications, facilitates justifications, and makes value judgments appear self-evident. And here again, it must be emphasised, truth is not of primary significance, but the communicative efficiency of stereotypes.

*

In view of the great importance of identity-creating narratives, the importance of *media* is obvious. The specificity of the different media defines in relevant ways what kinds of narratives can be told in what forms to what sets of addressees. The availability of media not only determines the range, storage and variability of identity-creating narratives (think only of the difference between oral and literal traditions), but also their position in the communication of a society as a whole. A society, in which, for example, everybody is familiar with an obligatory national epic, knows no problems of identity. Media societies with a multitude of competing 'national epics' find themselves in more difficult identity constellations because they have lost a classically integrative identity-instrument.

The basic pattern of conscious identity-formation is the same with regard to societal identity. Identity, therefore, arises for society members through the organising reference to the sequence of their references to themselves *as this particular society* in the form of narratives about who they are in contradistinction to others.

That the production and representation of social identity and personal identity is affectively charged as well as morally value-laden to a high degree, needs no further explanation. A drastic example for these relationships is provided by German post-war society whose identity problems remain acute and unsolved; for to this very day there is a gap of twelve years in the German autobiography, which requires explanation and justification, and which cannot be meaningfully closed. For the suppositions performed in those years, legitimate presuppositions have yet to be found — the very heart of the scandal.

12
Morality

Culture programmes regulate the socially acceptable references of agents to the model of reality of a society in a socially binding manner. In connection with the analysis of the conditions of communication, it was pointed out that the reflexivity of perception gave rise to two reflexive mechanisms: expectation-expectations in relation to what the partners in interaction and communication mutually attribute to each other as their so-called encyclopaedic knowledge or as world knowledge; and, imputation-imputations in relation to the motives, intentions, value orientations, and evaluations of the actions of the others.

Imputation-imputations, too, are systematised in every society; they serve every ego's orientation for self-assessment and the assessment of alter's actions, motives, attitudes and value orientations. Imputation-imputations regulate the spectrum of reflexive references to the evaluative assessment of given partner-images. The resulting, and effective, collective knowledge controls, by means of reflexivity, the references to the evaluations of actions and agents, and thus secures the social adequacy of such references by agents. Morality, it may now be stated in a preliminary attempt at definition, can be viewed as the dynamic order for collectively acceptable *evaluative* references to agents, actions and communications, in short, to all the components of histories.

Available, per reflexivity, as an operative fiction, morality deals with contingency in a contingent manner, and here again the contingency of this activity is rendered invisible to agents by the fact that the moral ordering principles function like blind spots in culture programmes. On this basis, actions in histories gain evaluation security, because in discourses the required justification of evaluative operations can always be successfully terminated by invoking the authority of moral orientation principles.

This double function of morality, rendering the *contingency of value orientations invisible,* and functioning as an *instance of interruption in legitimating discourses* for such value orientations, will be further elucidated in what follows.

*

If action, communication and identity presuppose the interaction with others, and in this way constitute the difference between alter and ego, then we are confronted by the problem of how the reflexive structure of relations between alter and ego, namely ego's image of alter and alter's image of ego, is to be socially regulated. In both cases the problem is, due to the logic of the preceding reflections, how one's own culturally programmed references to the model of reality and the references of the others can simultaneously be cognitively interpreted, affectively experienced, and morally evaluated. This evaluation, which 'co-occurs' in all actions and communications consciously or unconsciously, operates with a fundamental distinction that regulates the acceptance or the rejection of self-performed and other-performed actions, i.e. the distinction *good/evil*.

In the following, a concept will be explored, which models morality as the unity of the distinction between good and evil, or inclusion (respect) and exclusion (disrespect).

The argument will take care not to stumble into an ontological trap. This means that 'good' and 'evil' will be used as *attributes,* and will not, through nominalisation, be cast as the metaphysical chimaeras of the Good and the Evil. The decisive point of importance is what *we call and experience as* good and evil, and in what circumstances we use these attributes; it is not to declare what good and evil *is*.

As for the *genesis* of morality, the following hypothesis can be rendered plausible:

The reflexive reference of agents to each other is not only a cognitive and emotional challenge, it also perforce enacts an evaluation of any such reference by each and every agent. The elementary scale of social relevance for such evaluations is provided by the difference good/evil. As soon as the reflexive mechanism of distinguishing between good and evil had become internalised through evolution and socialisation, because everybody learned through communication that everything they did could be subjected to this evaluation, the recurrent standards of communication, which led to the application of the encoding of good vs. evil in actual cases, had also become lastingly internalised. At the same time, an affective reaction became associated with this internalisation, i.e. the reaction of shame. This means that whoever violated these internalised standards felt shame, even if their self-observation was not observed by others; for who really wanted to be evil and do evil? The moral orientations functioned extremely unobtrusively in the guise of operative fictions, i.e. once again as collective knowledge, attributed to all the others, with regard to the presupposed framework of interactive dependencies reality model&culture programme.

For this framework, the Christian religions, in particular, have developed a concept that is as vague as it is effective, namely the concept of 'conscience'. If the concept is separated from any reference to God, then one can say that conscience is the inner voice of those socialisation instances which reach our 'inner ear'. For this very reason alone, this voice is so compelling, because its message belongs amongst the unquestioned beliefs emerging during childhood and youth. It is certainly no accident that even today the public appeal to the conscience of agents is still an effective communication strategy.

The genesis of *individual* moral beliefs, in the form of the unquestioned adoption of moral precepts in childhood and youth, implies that morality 'is always already there', or that every single agent always arrives too late with regard to moral matters. Agents already possess 'a morality' and 'a conscience' before they can start to examine moral questions, because histories and discourses are pervaded by moral orientations regulating all forms of interactivity. Agents, however, can never return to a past prior to the inception of their histories and discourses. And therefore morality, unlike ethics, knows neither a beginning nor an end.

*

Moral precepts have evolved as principles of the (respectful) inclusion or (disrespectful) exclusion of actions and beliefs. The question behind the reasons for the genesis and the impact of social moral precepts can be answered as follows. Sociality arises through the enmeshing of reflexive structures. Agents, in the course of their reciprocal perception and (intended) observation, develop expectation-expectations with regard to mutually attributed knowledge, and imputation-imputations with regard to mutually attributed motives of action and communication in situations, in which different options can be selected or different decisions can be taken. In such situations, one ascribes to others the responsibility for selected options, because they could have decided otherwise; one knows or learns oneself, however, that the others do exactly the same. Responsibility must, however, have recourse to standards that are commonly accepted and followed, and about which communicative consensus can be achieved in histories and discourses. One could, therefore, put it briefly as follows: *Humans need morality because, and when, they act socially (i.e. reflexively with the help of operative fictions), and they act socially because, and when, they act morally, and the moral precepts are communicatively constituted, legitimated and modified.* Moral orientations are situational problem-solutions derived from an attitude of responsibility, which are justified in histories and discourses, and which are taken for granted by interaction partners of good will in histories&discourses. Further demands would have to use physical pressure to enforce obligations. H. von Foerster is therefore right in saying that it is not the end that justifies the means, but that the means justify the end.

Moral orientation principles may, consequently, be described as expectations of behaviours and evaluations in speech and action, which are shared by relevant societal groups in public discourse, which are affectively charged to a high degree, are communicatively and practically validated, and which all in all result from the experiential context of histories and discourses in which they are corroborated or transformed. Moral orientation principles may be recognised in all those patterns of interpretation for actions and communications, which agents in their life processes consider acceptable, normal, reasonable, typical, self-evident and mandatory for themselves and for others, and which can, therefore, on the basis of such societal evidence, be communicatively claimed by rights. Moral principles are what *is taken for granted* in a social group or in a society with regard to normative matters. One 'has' morality, it is inherent in action, it lives in life. One can therefore also say that morality tends to become a problem only in situations of conflict. If goodness is no matter for debate, business is as usual.

Moral precepts cannot only be treated and assessed from cognitive points of view, but also with regard to their *affective* and *moral* aspects. They possess a communicable semantic content resulting from the reference to the model of reality. As a rule, they are strongly charged affectively, because what is at stake is 'a tranquil conscience' as well as social inclusion or exclusion. And they are also automatically evaluated morally — one's own precepts are most definitely excellent, otherwise one would not follow them.

The interdependence of cognitive, affective and moral aspects of moral precepts manifests itself clearly in moral communication. Here, personalisation rules: immorality is personalised, morality depersonalised — there are the evil others, and there is goodness in itself. Emotions come necessarily into play whenever there is a question of inclusion or exclusion. Then — as already mentioned above — the violators of principles display shame and contrition and their accusers exasperation and superiority, not only on the verbal level but especially pungently also on the non-verbal level, i.e. with total communicative efficiency. In such situations, however, not all the available means are permitted, i.e. there is a societally mandatory morality for dealing with morality in moral communication, in order to avoid excesses of moral discourse.

*

Moral precepts form a particular component of the collective knowledge of the members of a society. In the realisation of actions they function like blind spots. Only in cases of conflict — as already mentioned — the (in)compatibility of actions and moral precepts becomes a topic of moral communication. Conflicts, i.e. situations in which the self-evidence of moral orientations is subjected to doubt, are occasions that can give rise to a new difference, namely the difference between morality as action according to confirmed principles, and *ethics* as the theory of the reflection of morality (according to N. Luhmann), which attempts to find general reasons for the justification of moral principles.

Such cases of conflict occur whenever there are *degrees of freedom* in a situation, i.e. different options for selection. An agent may then become uncertain as to which option to select, or an observer may blame him/her for having selected the wrong one — although one must be very careful to establish whether the agent saw, or was able to see, the same options as the observer. Conversely, this means: only where there are different options, i.e. where there is space for choice and correspondingly decisions can and must be taken, communication about morality begins, always and necessarily in a concrete framework of interactive dependencies histories&discourses. And it is precisely there that the moral-practical discourses about the correctness or acceptability of decisions take place, conducted by participants and victims alike, and with affirmed good arguments from all sides.

Whereas moral discourses concentrate on everyday goings-on in the life world, the mainstream of the *ethics debates* is largely context-abstract and is conducted under the auspices of a dualist, because observer-free, theory-design. Ethics to this day clings to the ideal of ultimate justification and the objectification and universalisation of values and norms. This is obviously only possible as long as agents and their always very concrete integration (enmeshedness) in histories and discourses are neglected. The claim to validity of ethical norms collides with the fact that ethics must unquestionably be fabricated by observers/agents in histories&discourses-based discourses in the context of actual distinction management, and that only then/afterwards can they be projected into a discourse of the other world. Ethics presents itself as the project of the ultimate theoretical immunisation of our moral beliefs in an other-worldly discourse. — This is perhaps the reason why it has been of so little consequence in the discourse of this world.

As N. Luhmann (1989, 1990) rightly noted, ethics never reflects its own blind spot, namely the apparently self-evident theoretical starting point with the difference good/evil. What about this difference itself, Luhmann asks, is it good or evil? And, one could continue, is this difference also applied in distinctions to ethics itself? Are theories of ethics necessarily either good or evil, or even both?

The ethics discourse has exhibited one constant feature since its beginnings: representatives of ethics have always entered the stage in order to end the debate about the justification of norms and values by means of a theory once and for all — provisional ethics theories are apparently considered as contradictions in themselves —, and they have failed to accomplish this task. By contrast, morality as the histories&discourses-bound application of moral orientation principles for the inclusion or exclusion of agents and their actions and communications, functions as a *pragmatic* interrupter of legitimation. This means that the recourse to collective knowledge, tradition, and viable societal judgment praxis, ultimately limits moral discourses to the task of restoring self-confidence and the reconstructing of damaged self-evident trivialities.

How can it then be explained that ethics fails as the theoretical interrupter of legitimation, whereas morality as the pragmatic interrupter of legitimation is definitely successful?

Ethics labours to create and justify norms of a universal kind, and these norms always take the time-independent form: You must always! It does not operate in the framework of histories&discourses where concrete principles of the moral conduct of life are dealt with, but forms its own framework of histories and discourses, in which moral criteria are abstracted from concrete cases in order to be generalised. In this way, however, ethics deprives morality and itself of their shared histories and discourses — and thus their common foundation.

Every observation of histories and discourses makes clear that norms, values and moral precepts are as indispensable in the domain of action and communication as truths in the domain of communicative action (see chapter 13). But just as *absolute* truths are not needed to make true statements, *absolute* norms, values and moral orientation principles are not needed to make actions socially calculable and justifiable. Moral precepts, like truths, must only be self-evident, plausible, consistent, and postulated with conviction in the moment of application or thematisation by agents and their observers. And that may hold equally well for 'local' as for absolute norms and precepts. Conflicts in the assessment of the validity of moral orientation principles can only arise between active and observing agents or between observers of the first and the second order. In such conflicts, both sides must be clearly aware that they are operating in different discourses and histories — which may make it impossible to settle their differences. In such situations a successful solution of problems can only be achieved if both parties manage to ascertain or develop, in the frame of a shared history, those moral orientation principles which can lead to a satisfactory problem solution, a solution that need not at all consist in consensus — heterogeneity in no way entails giving up interaction (see chapter 15).

Morality obviously functions precisely because it attempts to solve problems in histories and discourses temporarily. Ethics we need, at best, only as long as it helps us to endure competing ideas of morality by means of reflection.

The problem of moral conduct and moral communication in histories and discourses does not consist in 'breaking down' absolute norms to fit a given local situation, but in adapting to the moral orientation principles that have arisen in histories&discourses and have become accepted as mandatory in courses of actions in histories and discourses.

Our experience confirms the assumption introduced above that all our histories and discourses are pervaded by moral judgments to the last nook and cranny. We have an unquenchable desire to judge our own as well as other actions and communications immediately (at least tacitly) — even though we consciously want to abstain from any judgment. One may very well assume that this kind of concomitant evaluation plays an important role in the construction and stabilisation of identity through the establishment of differences that are valued as positive for the difference-maker. ('*I'd never* do a thing like that!')

Truths as well as moral precepts have developed historically in frameworks of histories&discourses and require legitimation. We cannot, therefore, speak of values in themselves, but only of values for ourselves. This 'ourselves' may refer to diverse aggregations; European society, for instance, may well have to realise that its conception of universal human rights is a specifically European one. In this connection the well-known problem arises that norms and values are part and parcel of the knowledge acquired in the process of socialisation, and are thus only partially observable and even only partly accessible to consciousness, because they belong — as already stated — among the blind spots of the processes of our reality construction. In any case, the point of origin for the observation, application and justification of values lies necessarily with us, and not with the others, nor in a discourse of the other world.

As moral problems involve the judgment of relations between human beings, the point of departure for all the arguments and decisions regarding ethics and morality is the *image of humanity* that, due to the presupposed epistemology, is implicitly or explicitly present in such contexts, and whose acceptance must — because of its inevitable consequences — be considered a moral decision.

If we uphold the hypothesis that all observation systems (here: all agents) are constantly busy with living their system-specific reality, then the position defended here has no choice but to introduce a double postulate of pluralism, i.e. a plurality of realities, and a plurality of values. Whoever wants to 'level' these pluralities theoretically, risks being caught up in a dualist position right from the start, which claims an observation point beyond observation, and thus access to absolute truth.

*

To conclude these deliberations, the expounded concept of morality as a pragmatic interrupter of legitimation will be brought into line with the previous argument.

Moral judgments are suppositions in histories&discourses, which subject not only the actions of others but also self-performed actions to a reference to the difference good/evil. Like all suppositions, such judgments follow presuppositions that, in cases of moral judgment, can be specified as the currently valid moral orientation principles within the relevant social reference group of the agent passing judgment. These principles synthesise the experiences of the reference group with regard to the hitherto viable difference management of good and evil and thus extend beyond the experiences of individual agents. In other words, in the reference to moral presuppositions, the individual agent also always arrives 'too late' — and this is probably the reason why this reference is socially mandatory.

Morality functions as the dynamic order guiding the evaluative reference to all moments of histories. These references are unceasingly taking place. Only irritations of these process-oriented references can generate the need to refer to such evaluative references by way of legitimation. These legitimating references are schematised, and thus stabilised, by morality. To put it differently: morality functions as an interrupter of legitimation, because it provides the common understanding of when and how to handle legitimating references.

In brief: morality successfully treats the contingency of the evaluative orientation of action in histories and discourses by rendering this contingency culturally invisible. Like consciousness, communication and culture, morality is always taken for granted, and made use of, whenever morality is discussed. Morality is involved in everything we do, as is postulated by the concept of the model of reality introduced here, with its five dimensions including morality (see chapter 2). One can therefore rightly say that morality is auto-constitutive; for good action obeys moral orientation principles, and these principles result from good action.

Moral discourses interrupt moral action and, through reflexivity, permit the formation of structures in the form of the conscious difference management of good and evil, but admit of no absolute justification of any kind. This difference management must take into account that the guiding difference good/evil, in its application in histories and discourses, factually follows the semantics of *responsible/irresponsible*, because it is the consequences connected with good/evil that are of prime importance here. This means that what is of interest is not the reference to universally valid values and norms, but the plausibly argued responsibility for the consequences of particular actions. Responsibility one can, however, only shoulder for calculable sequences of actions. One is therefore confronted by a well-known twofold problem. On the one hand, agents can assess only those consequences which they can recognise in a given context, and by virtue of their own observational capacities, and they may therefore have to enter into conflicts with other agents who, due to their histories and discourses, view those consequences quite differently. On the other hand, one must distinguish between intended and unintended consequences of actions. As one can shoulder responsibility only for predictable consequences, the only thing that can be demanded of consequence assessment is that agents act to the best of their knowledge and in good conscience, i.e. morally. This means, however, that the difference good/evil finds its practical moral correlative in the difference responsible/irresponsible.

The actual moral orientation principles of a particular society deal with universal contingency which involves irrevocable compulsory selection, by means of specific contingency, i.e. through developing and complying with sectoral or local evaluation principles. In this way, it becomes possible to achieve success in moral discourses as well as in decision situations by wisely relinquishing the demand for universal categories (or corresponding obligations). This renunciation of an (only in dualist theories) indispensable postulate of absolute values makes anti-fundamentalist moral decisions in concrete histories and discourses accessible to compromise — or as wise as observers of the second order can be and should be.

If agents are only capable of acting responsibly for themselves, then there can only be — as H. von Foerster repeatedly emphasised — an 'I-want-ethics' and no 'you-must-ethics', because agents must respect the freedom of others by making use of their own freedom (whether desired or not). This I-want-ethics is called an implicit attitude by von Foerster. However, through structural coupling with other agents, it is transformed into a dialogical (communicative) attitude, which — following the argument — leads to the creation of eigenvalues, i.e. produces social eigenbehaviour.

The commandment of tolerance, resulting from the attitude of responsibility, has as a correlative on the part of agents both the duty to justify moral decisions in cases of conflict, and the duty to reform their behaviour in the case of acknowledged wrongdoing, independently of whether there is criticism by observers or not. The justification here again follows the guiding difference responsible/irresponsible and must, in any case, include the agent involved in the argument. In moral discourses as well as in decision situations requiring moral justification, there is no neutral outsider position, there are only participants, all enmeshed in histories, who are, whatever they do, 'evaluating beings'.

13

Truth

The problem of truth is again best approached with reference to the two fundamental problems of mankind, which have already been mentioned several times: the problem of the auto-constitution of selectivity and contingency, and the problem of the mediation between cognitive autonomy and social orientation. And here again, as in the other cases discussed up to now, the point of interest is the treatment of the problem of contingency by means of reflexivity.

*

Expectation-expectations, as has been stressed repeatedly, evolve as a form of reference to the encyclopaedic knowledge, or 'world knowledge', that is attributed to others. From this source the collective knowledge arises that moulds all assertoric discourses, i.e. all the discourses specified by statements. The communicative co-orientation of others can only succeed by reference to the actively available knowledge attributed to them. In order to achieve and guarantee semantic reliability (correct language) and statement reliability (correct reference), such knowledge must be given a label that is inseparable from it in thought and can be made the basis of claims by rights in cases of conflict, and this label is *truth*.

Truth is defined as the unity of the difference *true/false*. Truth, as statement reliability in histories and discourses, renders the contingency of everything known invisible, and serves as the interrupter of arguments by virtue of the legitimacy of the reference to the *status quo* of shared knowledge. Moreover, there is the requirement that, following the conclusion of an argument, a renewed corroboration of truth can be demanded any time, which should not, as a rule, be refused. In other words, querying is part of the dignity of the truth discourse, it is, as it were, its morality.

This basic mechanism will now be further elucidated.

*

True can only be what can also be false, P. Janich (1996) emphasises. Correspondingly, *truth* refers to elements of discourse, to statements, assertions, and arguments, but not to objects and matters of fact. By labelling statements and assertions as *true*, we intend to solve temporarily both the starting and the finishing problem in communication processes and discourses. Instead of undertaking a futile attempt to start with absolute primordial reasons, we inevitably begin by falling back on already existing consensual knowledge, i.e. by recourse to knowledge that has been confirmed cognitively and communicatively, and has therefore already been labelled as true. And we can, on the other hand, terminate our arguments and their justifications as soon as we have reached an (explicit or implicit) consensus through the discourse in corresponding histories. In other words: since we cannot, for simple pragmatic reasons, infinitely continue to harbour doubts, we must be able to interrupt the regress of justification arising from our doubts in a consensually acceptable way, and this interruption must be accorded high social reputation so as not to be shrugged off as pure wilfulness. Both conditions are sufficiently fulfilled by the concept 'truth'.

Truth is *ascribed* to statements and systems of statements if *we,* on the basis of the state of our knowledge and, consequently, on the basis of successful previous experiences, see good reasons to consider them as true. The sort of knowledge one can appeal to without objection in an argumentatively connectible context, that sort of knowledge is held to be true knowledge. (This is why knowledge, according to N. Luhmann, is always associated with an implicit claim to truth.) Truth is, correspondingly, always carrying an (at least implicit) time-index: statement p is true if p conforms with our present unquestioned knowledge; and, truth refers to socially different sets of knowledge and rules of attribution of the predicate 'true': p is true for all those who, in their own histories and discourses, refer to the same kind of knowledge, and who attribute this reference to all others. In other words, truth is enacted as the functioning reflexivity of knowledge evaluation in discourse. As with 'culture', we could say here: 'the truth' does not exist, but we need truth ascription as an indispensable controller of discourse.

A statement designated as true represents, correctly and reliably, our state of knowledge qua cognitively interpreted experience. In this sense—i.e. not from within itself—it is evident, and can therefore be formulated in corresponding statements and assertions, as if it were independent of time and agents and resistant to histories&discourses. For this reason, the designation 'true' functions as a powerful discourse instrument for its user and may easily lead to the belief that truth is something one can possess, and 'not just' a discourse controller.

Statements and assertions take place in discourses embedded in histories. They are enacted, i.e. belong to the category 'action', and can as such succeed or fail, reach or miss goals. Like all actions, they follow action schemata and are acquired communally in the course of socialisation(s). Assertions, as actions, P. Janich maintains, are not only dependent on comprehension but also on agreement, something that is decisive for the truth of an assertion. Janich, therefore, defines truth as assertoric success, asserting being not just a mere talking description of the world, but a means of the organisation of communal praxis, whose truth is endorsed by the successful accomplishment of the actions initiated in its course. Like identity and morality, truth is also a product of attribution, requiring the agreement of all the participants involved in the relevant attribution process, and is certainly not just an attitude open to choice that can be individually chosen or rejected.

The communicatively realised operation of the assessment of a description, explanation or interpretation as 'true', as a rule, clandestinely brings about the tacit elimination of the observer, a situation expressed succinctly by an aphorism of the Austrian writer F. J. Czernin: '*truth*: what forbids us to think, whenever we assert something, that we are mentioning ourselves at the same time.' For this same reason, discourses about the truth of truths should be consistently conducted from the perspective of an observer of the second order, so that contingency is necessarily *rendered visible*.

Truth, according to H. von Foerster (1993), is the invention of a liar. This is to mean: truth, as a category of discourse, is only needed whenever doubts arise, whenever we feel cognitively unwell, whenever actions fail. Truth is a creature of conflict, a category of the observer of the second order. Because we cannot tell ourselves the truth, as the writer R. Walser once pithily noted, our doubts are usually cast upon the statements of others, and from the conflict between ours and their beliefs, our own beliefs, as a rule, emerge victorious — because we hold them to be true. The strategy behind all that has been expressed by J. Mitterer in the formula that truth (like morality) is de-personalised, and falsehood is, by contrast, personalised: 'the truth' is always on our side, 'false' are always the statements of the others. And as all those, who can and may advance claims to truth in discourse, which can be discursively realised, possess at least reputation if not power, it becomes clear that truth, beside morality, functions as an important mechanism of socio-cultural differentiation.

*

In an observer- and process-oriented, non-dualist argument, the attribution of the category 'true/truth' is, consequently, seen as a *discourse strategy* that helps to determine the communicative quality of statements, i.e. their success in action, not, however, their congruence with something existing outside themselves, as in most of the correspondence theories of truth. 'Communicative quality' may here refer to quite different things, depending on the discourse: discursive success (connectibility), usefulness, degree of assent, force of conviction, authenticity, evidence, conformity, coherence, consistency etc. The emphatic concept of truth, as promoted by dualist philosophies, appears to be especially attractive because it is evidently concerned with *power* and the rejection of dialogue and responsibility — from science and religion to politics, education, and partner relations. Those holding the view that one can be 'in possession of the truth', however, commits a twofold mistake: they assume that truth is something existing in itself, i.e. something independent of time and person; but at the same time they postulate the ability to claim possession of this something through time- and person-dependent histories and discourses, and thus escape the contingency of histories and discourses by entering a 'discourse of the other world' (in the sense of J. Mitterer). In a non-dualist discourse, truth does not figure in the singular or as an entity, but only in the plural and in the adjectival form of the application of the difference true/false. The recent attempts by many authors to tie truth once again to experiences of perceptual evidence, are therefore expressly rejected here, because perception (as explained in chapter 1) is seen here as a process of reference by observers, and not as a representation of reality.

Accepted statements that can be condensed into expectations (structures), exhibit their truth-quality by way of consonance, i.e. by fitting into the ensemble of experiences that agents have made in connection with such statements in their previous histories&discourses. This consonance derives from compatibility with the standards of normality constituted in the model of reality and the culture programme, which, like a system of blind spots, constitute the profile of self-evident knowledge of a society — socially mandatory, and independent of individual agents. We cannot, therefore, strictly speaking, postulate truth as our goal, because we always already possess it, i.e. in the form of our knowledge and our beliefs in histories&discourses. Put differently: with regard to the knowledge of truth, we always inevitably arrive *too late*, the production of truth from knowledge is always ahead of us.

*

The handling of the truth attribute can be differentiated into a cognitive and a communicative aspect.

In cognitive processes, we treat statements practically as true for as long as the process of meaning construction by means of the semiotic materiality of the statements is neither irritated nor interrupted. The presumption of truth is enacted here as an experience of immediate evidence. As long as the cognitive process of order creation is running undisturbed, the question of truth does not arise; we approve what we receive. If the process is interrupted, then we raise the question by communicating with ourselves, as it were, whether and why we are convinced by the meaning construct that we have assigned to the statement within the context of our available knowledge, or whether we can envisage a scenario that can support our belief (e.g. documents, methods of proof, statements by witnesses, experiments).

In communicative processes, too, as already stated, the question of truth does not arise as long as the process is not interrupted, and statements, assertions or arguments are not called into question or subjected to doubt. Here the recourse to true statements functions as an interrupter of legitimation, which restores the connectibility of communication. The ascription of truth realises itself here as a decision scenario, in which those knowledge constellations or decision practices are adduced which, at the given state of discourse, are accepted without protest.

*

Is there, beside the reference of truth to discourse, also a *reference to histories*?

As already suggested above, the tacit ascription of truth to our discourse-related knowledge has the effect of rendering the contingency of this knowledge invisible—trust reigns. We act as if we were in 'possession of the truth'— until a conflict changes our view for the better. In order to avoid equivocation, I therefore propose to use, as the equivalent of 'truth' in relation to histories, E. von Glasersfeld's concept of *viability*. Viability, or practicality, designates successful problem solution. An action is viable if it is successful in histories and discourses, and the action success is assessed 'culturally' (according to P. Janich) by agents according to their criteria of expectation and assessment in their given histories-framework.—And because agents are conservative systems, they will only make alterations if the utility test, in the sense of successful action, has failed at least once. (In most cases, agents are more patient.)

This proposal rests on the following argument. If truth is not designed in the mode of correspondence relations (reality and knowledge, statement and object), but as the cognitively and communicatively efficient strategy of the invisibly contingent treatment of contingency, then it can be specified, from the observational perspective 'discourse', as the successful communication, stabilisation, and regress interruption, that permits communal action; and from the observational perspective 'history', as the social assessment of an action as a viable problem solution, in the sense of a successful coupling with the environment in a social context. In both cases, in histories as in discourses, the goal is action success. If there is—as P. Janich also emphasises in his reflections on truth—an indissoluble interdependence between actions and assertions, then successful action becomes the definiens of 'action-truth'. Assertions intended to serve as instruments of successful problem solutions must be true, if they are to be suitable for the organisation of communal praxis. The lack of action success renders assertions false; for assertions, as true speech, function as a summons in the organisation of communal activity.

Truth, too, as a strategy of contingent contingency treatment, integrates cognitive, affective and moral aspects. Unquestioned acceptable knowledge permits cognitive and communicative operation, and allows for a positive pleasure-pain-equilibration (in the sense of L. Ciompi). To command true knowledge is emotionally satisfying. In everyday life — apart from special forms of communication like humour or advertising — it is morally expected (however counterfactually) that every agent always speaks the truth — white lies are the utmost in excusable counteraction. And scientists, in particular, are under high moral pressure to create and spread true, and only true, knowledge, unless they want to risk losing their reputation. Conversely, in fulfilling this expectation, they gain both cognitive and emotional satisfaction as well as social recognition.

*

How are we to deal with *logical truths*?

Logical truths can be equated with the rule-conforming application of logical operations for the purpose of categorising and conceptualising experiences. It must, however, not be overlooked here that systems of logic are our own achievement, invented, applied and interpreted throughout the course of time in histories&discourses. (Compared with the statement calculus, for instance, modal logic is still a recent invention.) It would, therefore, be highly implausible to want to transfer logical systems to an extra-worldly sphere of validity, i.e. to an other world beyond histories and discourses, no matter whether one interprets logical truths as necessities or as objective truths.

And finally, what about the so highly esteemed *scientific truths*? According to the line of argument pursued so far, only pragmatic truth strategies are acceptable for scientific statements and the system of science as a whole. The reason lies in the conception of science as a specific societal organisation (form) for the cultural production of cognitive semantic order (knowledge). This order arises only in/as relation to observers and their presupposition-rich distinctions. In the scientific production of knowledge we thus observe only the success of the intersubjective application of our own principles of order creation, which we interpret other-referentially as soon as they are accepted by relevant (groups of) agents. Successful reflexivity lends truth to the order created. Whether this success is accredited 'by nature', is again a question that only we ourselves can answer.

Truth is, therefore, specified once again as a controlling idea that obliges scientists to pursue specific ideals of action, and this obligation must, at the same time, be understood as a moral obligation to truth. Here again the appropriate question is not what scientific truth *is*, but what follows from the fact that scientists *accept* statements as true — for only acceptance ascribes truth to statements and simultaneously responsibility for the consequences of their acceptance *as* truth.

In the context of his hypothesis that the sciences are up-graded practices of human lifeworlds, P. Janich unequivocally defines scientific truth as *action success*. Scientific problem solutions are, due to their methodical control, amenable to intersubjective and interdisciplinary discourse, i.e. their performance power for particular purposes can be argued explicitly. The connection with action is clearly evident in the experiment-based empirical truths that are valid only in relation to the acceptance of the norms governing the ways in which the apparatuses used in experiments are invented, fabricated and operated. Truth may therefore be typified descriptively in correspondence with the conditions of its production.

Apart from the production of scientific results, their presentation is no less subject to logical truth expectations; but even logics cannot — as emphasised above — pave a royal road to 'the truth', they provide instructions for consistent argumentation that may vary considerably between different areas of application. Logics also have their histories and discourses.

The philosophy of science has so far failed to come up with generally accepted truth criteria. Spotlighting the production and presentation of scientific truths in the special discourses of the sciences reveals, however, that there are indeed commonly accepted guidelines for successful scientific action, e.g. the theory-orientation of empirical research, the explicitness of theories and terminologies, the operationalisation of problem-solving, the intersubjectivity of testing knowledge production, the explicitness of result presentation etc.

The procedures of truth testing exclusively employ cognition-immanent criteria, i.e. indicators that make an ascription of truth acceptable, and such indicators are obtained through the instrumentalisation or methodical ordering of courses of action. The potential satisfaction of truth criteria can then be specified as the operational effectiveness of a theory for predictions. And the criteria of operativity are actually decidable, namely by the observation of consequences, effects etc. in the experiential reality of the observer.

*

Focussing on the difference between lifeworldly and scientific truth productions, makes the following obvious: for observers of the first order who, with good reasons, operate in their life-praxis as if they were philosophical realists, no truth-theoretical complications will arise (except in cases of conflict). Their concept of truth follows the semantics of 'correct', 'fits', 'matches my own experiences', 'credible', or 'probably okay'. There are various ways of testing the truth of statements (in the sense of: acceptance in the context of the knowledge system of other observers): checking oneself, interviewing witnesses, inquiry with experts, demanding documentary evidence etc. A statement remains true as long as nothing is known to the contrary. Accepting a statement usually does not imply an examination of the relation between facts and statement, but simply consists in signalling assent, since the actual checking of the relation is only possible in exceptional cases.

Whereas the genesis of our cognitive procedures through sensorimotor-cognitive operations and their abstraction (in the sense of J. Piaget) does not (necessarily) play a role with regard to our ordinary-language concept of truth, it is definitely of relevance on an epistemological level. A processually conceived truth concept must, therefore, take into account the genesis of our knowledge-producing strategies in order to avoid representationist conceptualisations. If we properly appreciate that the production of knowledge and order presupposes knowledge and order, then coherence can be specified as the correspondence of different kinds of knowledge amongst themselves as well as with the total system of knowledge pertaining to a particular discourse. On this basis, J. D. Sneed's proposal to design and assess knowledge on the level of the sciences as theory-true or discourse-true, seems convincing.

Disregarding the fact that 'truth' is rarely talked about in the daily business of science — what matters there is whether a hypothesis is plausible, a research result interesting, or an experiment successful —, the discussion of truth in scientific discourses deals with the maintenance of obligatory rules of discourse, consensual (intersubjectively applicable, i.e. operational) practices of knowledge production and presentation, connectibility in communication etc. The science system, as N. Luhmann (1990a) emphasises, moulds itself. It is, therefore, vital to observe when and how the agents within this system deal with truth attributions in histories and discourses and what the consequences are.

*

The fact that the truth discourse is so strongly tied to science and philosophy, often blocks out the perception of other domains of society that have developed and cultivated their own truth discourses, e.g. religion and art, but also (increasingly) politics or business. When the rising social system of science had, by the 18th century, successfully managed to reserve an epistemically 'hard', subject-free, truth concept for itself, all the other social systems were forced to re-code their own truth semantics, and thus a cultural pluralisation of truth concepts took place (leading to religious, political, artistic truths, but also to the truth of reporting in the thriving journalism of the period).

For every single truth concept asserting exclusiveness (i.e. excluding functional equivalents), a triple claim was put forward, an epistemic one, a moral one, and a claim to power; whoever was 'in possession' of truth, knew more than others, was morally superior and therefore entitled to educate and lead others — and that usually meant: take charge of them.

Religion and art adopted, and retain, a special position. The truth concept of religion had a personal reference (God and revelation), and religion was, consequently, transcendently based and unassailable. Art postulated the world-internal epiphany of world-external values like beauty, eternity, or Being, in the perfect work of art.

The legal system took, and still occupies, a quite differently connoted exceptional position. On the one hand, it had to come to terms with the experience that all the attempts of an objective justification or derivation of legal norms (from God, nature, or tradition) have failed. On the other hand, every judge, in every new case, proposes to undertake finding out 'the truth'. And in contradistinction to the lecture theatre, where truth-oriented discourse is tacitly presupposed, the courtroom is the only place where agents are publicly and by oath enjoined 'to tell the truth and nothing but the truth', although everybody knows that the persons under oath can only state what they hold to be true to the best of their knowledge and in good conscience.

To tell the truth — always and under any circumstances — is one of the moral precepts of 'our culture'. It entails the presumption that everybody, when speaking, actually knows what the truth is and is, furthermore, in a position to decide whether to tell it or not. However, the sentence 'knows the truth' has many readings, e.g. knowing what the time is, what the price of the car was, whether the trip really stopped at Timbuktu, whether the trial runs did indeed yield identical results without a single exception, or whether snow is white. Should someone ask speakers with reference to such cases whether they were actually telling the truth or not, they must have a reason for doing so (lack of trust, possession of conflicting information, doubts concerning speaker intentions etc.).

It is therefore always of value to observe as precisely as possible who poses the *question of truth* in what situation and with what intention. With this question, the transition from an emphatic to a contingent and pragmatic (process-oriented) conception of truth is completed. There are many good arguments for such a histories&discourses-oriented conception of truth, except one — *the truth.*

14

Interim Summary 3

How can the postulated interdependence of identity, morality, and truth be specified more precisely?

The formation and maintenance of identity possesses both an action aspect and a communication aspect. Identity ascription presupposes that agents show moral continuity in their actions, and that they 'stick to the truth' in the communicative presentations of their identities. Their morality must be in keeping with the true knowledge of their evaluation community, and the morality of truth-oriented communication demands that, in principle, 'the truth be told' at all times.

By enmeshing the important reflexive mechanisms of identity, morality, and truth, societies, in the course of their evolution, transform universal contingency, i.e. the insecurity of identity, morality, and truth, into well-founded constructions, into *stable contingency*, as it were. Identity ascription refers to the fulfilment of the expectations of communicative and moral authenticity of agents, moral orientation-orientation refers to the fulfilment of the expectations of the principles of their morally good life conduct, and communicative truth ascription refers to the reliability of their references to the given state of the reflexively attributed undisputed knowledge. Therefore, morality and truth can, for the agents in societies, render contingency invisible, function as interrupters of legitimation for orientation principles (values), and as interrupters of justification regresses for truths (certainties), without potential or necessary recourse to 'the good' or 'the truth'. To all three domains applies what S. Jünger has marked out as a feature of identity, namely the continuity of change as the change of continuity.

These exemplary reflections on identity, morality, and truth were intended to supplement the deliberations on process-dependent realities in order to show that not only 'the order of things' and 'the order of words' can be presented as results of generative reflection processes, but also 'the order of relations' and 'the order of values'. The intention was to show that it is not only possible but advisable to argue non-dualistically in these domains, and that one may thereby disconnect oneself from the continuity of those European problem designs which deal with identity, morality, and truth in an identity-theoretical way, instead of by way of difference theory and process orientation.

The concepts gained by following this course have the additional advantage that they are not normative ones, and that they are, furthermore, abstract enough to allow for the explication of quite different problems in the three concept dimensions regarding their individual and social aspects. Furthermore, the derivation of these concepts demonstrates their intrinsic interdependence, which results from their function of order formation and helps considerably to render them invisible.

15

Why a Theory of Histories&Discourses?

There is certainly no lack of rival theories on the discourse market of philosophy and science. It is, therefore, advisable to raise the question of the need for a new theoretical proposal oneself before others prepare to do so. The assessment of the rationale offered will have to be left to others, anyway.

*

It was already explained in chapter 9 why it makes sense to dissolve some of the persistent problems of European philosophy, created unnaturally as they were by dualistic reasoning — to show the fly the way out of the fly bottle, as it were, to quote L. Wittgenstein. In European thought, the problems in question definitely possess the status of 'grand' philosophical problems, e.g. the problems of reality, of truth, of the representational adequacy of knowledge, of the universal validity of values, of the reference of language or the true foundation of philosophical theorising. I have attempted to demonstrate that all these problems appear to result from the same unreflected starting manoeuvre: frameworks of interactive dependencies are broken up into components by means of these very frameworks, these components are then separated from their constitutive frameworks and treated as independently existing entities — from which basis philosophical thinking takes off. Due to this unreflected starting manoeuvre, dualistic philosophical thinking generates the dichotomies it has been toiling with for centuries, e.g. the dichotomies of subject and object, reality and knowledge, statement and truth, individual and society, or society and culture.

In opposition to this line of approach, the idea will be promoted that consciousness, observation and description clearly are the blind spots of our 'reality construction', and that we are only too willing to forget that we can only see and know anything at all solely with their support. The strategy of argument pursued by non-dualistic philosophical thinking, therefore, consists in disturbing the smooth service of these blind spots, in order to show that entities 'exist' only in the reference of consciousness, objects only as objects in descriptions, order only as system-specific synthesis etc.

The dissolution of the problems of dualistic philosophical thinking by the deliberate shifting of the starting manoeuvre from objects to processes and their conditions, provides two insights:

- It reminds us that we ourselves have made these problems so grand and apparently irresolvable, because we have, in the shadow of our blind spots, quasi absconded from the history of problem invention. As a consequence, *our* problems loom giant-like above us as if they had sprung from the other (discourse) world, larger than life, instead of arising from our own cognitions and communications. (And even if they were ghosts *we* would have had to invoke

them, in order to render ourselves unable to get rid of
them again.)
- It makes us aware that there can be no emphatic,
  unconditional beginning for philosophical reflection
  or any other kind of theorising, but only a start. As we,
  as human beings, always arrive too late with regard to
  all the relevant concerns, from consciousness to language and culture, our theory-starts are nothing but
  transitions, which are perpetuated by reflection, and
  thus given relevance *for us*.

A further justification for the usefulness of the theory presented is, in my view, that it has to do with the focused testing of two simple strategies. On the one hand, the strategy of gaining knowledge through *observational variance,* which was demonstrated, for instance, by the systematic application of the variance process/sense-orientation in relation to a theory of action and communication; on the other hand, the strategy of exploring how far the tested line of argument will carry, which led to the discovery of a remarkable number of self-justifying complementarities (see the glossaries in the appendix).

Non-dualistic philosophical thinking, thirdly, secures human-scale problem-*dimensioning* and resistance against fundamentalisms of all sorts. We talk about true and false 'culturally', because we need regress-interrupters for contexts of argument. However, the premise here is not whether we have approximated 'the truth' or even taken possession of it, but whether we attribute the predicate 'true' meaningfully, and what function this manoeuvre fulfils in different kinds of discourse. In cases of conflict, we pose the question culturally as to whether someone's action was good or evil. However, to answer this question, we do not consider the case from the perspective of 'the Good', but with reference to those moral beliefs that we, *rebus sic stantibus*, hold to be (in-)compatible with our moral standards, these socio-culturally and socio-historically grown beliefs serving, at the same time, as acceptable legitimation-interrupters. It is not 'the Good' or 'the Truth' that enforce the moral and semantic order in our histories&discourses, but *reflexivity* as the mechanism generating every kind of communalisation and sociality. Without the reference to social orientations, as they are provided by the operative fiction of collective knowledge and enable us, in spite of our cognitive autonomy, to interact and communicate, we would need neither truth nor morality, nor even any kind of biographical order and identity as ascribed to ourselves through social attribution.

*

Non-dualistic philosophical thinking within a theory of histories&discourses also contributes to a 'more realistic' appreciation of our knowledge and our sciences. N. Luhmann (1990a) rightly pointed out that knowledge is, by and large, automatically associated with truth. We hold our knowledge to be true — what else could we possibly do. And as we do not constantly pursue it with distrust, we rarely notice that, and how, it keeps changing, how unpredictably it is distributed over societal groups, societies or cultures, how it is partially declining (e.g. the knowledge of crafts, the knowledge of medicinal plants etc.), or how it is being re-valued. We tend to overlook, owing to the auto-constitution of positing and presupposing, that there can be no knowledge without action in histories&discourses related to the framework of interactive dependencies reality model&culture programme, nor any action without knowledge (and that, too, is an argumentative necessity). Action

Why a Theory of Histories&Discourses? 165

leads to knowledge, knowledge to capability. With these considerations, a theory of histories&discourses gives strength to the argument that it is the intrinsic framework of action, knowledge and capability, which defines what, and how, we know, a framework that, due to the bodyhood of humans, integrates cognitive, affective, and moral components into a relationship of mutual attraction. For this reason, the action-character of perceiving, knowing or describing must be adequately taken into account, because these are all praxes that are culturally styled and take place within histories and discourses. Only by way of analysis can bodily aspects be separated from mental and spiritual ones. The interface between agent and reality, therefore, lies not in perceptions, knowledge or languages, but in actions, in the concrete embodiment of actual perceiving, knowing and communicating within a concrete framework of interactive dependencies of histories&discourses in relation to reality model&culture programme.

From such a perspective, science appears as a special societal histories&discourses-framework for the production of special, i.e. theoretically and methodologically controlled, forms of knowledge. The need for such forms of knowledge arises, as an agent-bound need for problem-solving, both inside and outside the sciences, and thus also regulates the relevant modalities of the application of such forms of knowledge. If *we* have no problems for which we can evaluate successful solutions, we could paraphrase Carl Friedrich von Weizsäcker a third time, then there can be no question of *problems*.

*

Non-dualistic philosophical thinking leaves the emphatic question of 'the' reality behind and concentrates on the questions of how realities arise in our actions and what we can and may do with them. Here again, cognitive, affective and moral aspects become indissolubly linked. We debate what kinds of realities the media can or may produce and how we can and may use such products. We worry about the realities generated by biology and medicine, nano-technology and computer-technology, and how best to deal with such new realities. As long as we, when confronted by such developments, do not lose sight of the simple fact that such realities can neither arise nor be made use of without human beings, then the discourse about our realities, for one, will make us aware of our very own responsibility and block the escape route of shoving off our responsibility onto 'the reality', and, secondly, it will urge us to develop creativity in the generation and the management of new realities, instead of merely staring at it as the *non plus ultra* of givenness.

*

Finally, non-dualistic philosophical thinking can help us to solve some of the problems of multiculturalism and globalisation. If culture, as explained above, is modelled as a programme for successful difference-management, i.e. both as the problem-solving memory and as the problem-solving design of a society, then it can at once be taken for granted that cultures do not differ according to superior or inferior quality but solely according to the complexity and social viability of their problem-solving. By means of culture programmes, a society solves precisely those problems which it considers relevant and, at the same time, evaluates both problems and solutions affectively and morally. It follows that *every* culture programme is selective and thus contingent, a specific form of improbability, by means of which societies system-specifically select and interpret their environmental relations. Cultural globalisation can, therefore, succeed up to the extent that partial programmes and modes of application of different culture programmes can be globalised. Increasingly, it is the media that permit the observation of the impact and the influences of other culture programmes. Transculturalism, as the potential mode of cultural existence of a globalised media-society, can then be specified as the acceptance of difference without relinquishing one's own identity.

A theory of histories&discourses can contribute considerably to the explication and differentiation of this thematic complex.

Of great importance is here the fundamental insight that all reference is system-specific. It entails that difference, heterogeneity, and plurality have to be seen as culturally programmed phenomena, and not as problems or even calamities. In this observational perspective the terror that contingency may spread does not dominate perception. The primary concern is much rather the creative possibilities of contingency treatment.

Whoever accepts difference, heterogeneity, and plurality, may very well hope to change conditions, because these conditions can, as they have been made by humans, (only) be changed by humans. Furthermore, for them tolerance will not be a particularly taxing moral commandment, but a form of recognising everyone's right to their very own kind of life.

The conception of culture as a programme of problem-solving facilitates the conceptual separation of culture and nation and allows the creation of models for concepts of multi- and transculturalism. In this way, not only the difference global/local is served, and not just by the terminological neologism 'glocal', but transparent reasons are given for the need for problem-solving programmes on all levels of meaningful social communalisation. The fact, for instance, that tribal law is valid and actually applied alongside state law both in the United States of America and in many African states, is therefore no anthropologists' quirk. Similarly, the so-called global players in the economic domain have to consider very carefully in which spheres their subsidiaries in other countries will need to apply their own (partial) culture programmes.

A theory of histories&discourses will, finally, permit a more flexible handling of the question as to whether there can be something like culture without consensus, or peaceful controversy without solution, or globalism without unification. The general answer here is that the basic strangeness embodied by every single human being qua system-specificity of all reference in histories and discourses, makes cooperation by way of selective diversity even without general consensus the 'normal case', anyway. If, however, all and everything are different, then it is impossible to wait with cooperative action until total unity and empathic understanding have been reached. On the contrary, common action will be required to create something like partial unity among the participants, and its meaning will then become evident in practice. The point here is that giving up on consensus must not be equated with giving up on interaction and communication. Therefore, processes of self-organisation will have to be encouraged for purely practical reasons, in order to initiate developments the course and end of which cannot be predicted, so that planned and unplanned, causally governed and circular-causal, interactive processes can be utilised for purposes of cooperation. And equally for practical reasons, forms of the strategic use of operative fictions will have to be explored, which may help to build up networks without basic consensus. (Many consider Switzerland as a genuinely existing example of such a strategy for the peaceful regulation of pluralisms.)

*

The question of *power*, notorious in (post)modern discourse, can be answered by a theory of histories&discourses in the following way: apart from the constitutionally established domains of power, from politics, security and defence to business and administration, a multitude of possibilities for the emergence and execution of power exists. Power possesses and wields who determines by means of which distinctions socially relevant problems are dealt with, e.g. the inclusion or exclusion of societal groups. (Cultural Studies have analysed numerous pertinent examples.) Power possesses and wields who can supply key concepts in memory-political discourses, who can ascribe understanding or misunderstanding to others, who can accept or reject images of identity, who can establish stereotypes or forbid humour, who admits or prevents contributions to discourses, who is allowed to pose questions of truth or renounce moral consensus, who can decide about the career of topics of debate and launch images. Consequently, the discourse of power must be considerably differentiated further, and this differentiation can be guided by the question of who finally manages to win the battle of the difference management with regard to societally relevant problems.

*

It may be objected against observational variance and the hierarchisation of observation as methods (Hilary Putnam has done so, for instance) that permanent observing of the second order is ill-advised, as it may disturb agents and put them under mental stress.

This council was probably wise in times when latent observation was the special competence of philosophers. In media-culture societies with highly differentiated media systems, the observation of observers, as N. Luhmann already noted, has become daily praxis. Media systems observe observers and observe each other, sometimes even themselves when observing.

In this situation everything will depend on how societies handle the growing consciousness of contingency. To prevent people from escaping into apparently alleviating fundamentalisms, it must be made clear in public discourses that contingency can be successfully and even creatively treated without finalities, if the different modes of mainly implicit societal contingency treatment, as they have been described in this book, are deliberately and purposively applied. The acceptance of specific contingency may significantly advance the appreciation of democracy and its requirement to achieve solutions by compromise, it may even enhance the creativity of new problem solutions by making clear that the so-called factual constraints are, in fact, self-generated. The insight into our contingent condition is, therefore, not at all a momentary glimpse into the abyss, but much rather the realisation of our proper view of the reality we, and we alone, are responsible for — the abyss after all?

*

A theory of histories&discourses can also make us more resistant to disappointment. Having taken account of the dissolutions of problems and the insights into our belatedness, as demonstrated by this theory, one can accept the thesis of the finality of contingency with no feeling of loss. Our discourses are indeed bottomless and interminable. They are determined — apart from all the praiseworthy factual arguments — by emotions, traditions, habits or *habitus*, which function like blind spots. If they are interesting enough, they may give rise to the emergence of discourse communities, which reveals something about their success but nothing about their truth.

The upshot of these considerations, 'the finality of transience', is therefore a consoling, a mitigating formula which, however, would be incomplete without its converse, 'the transience of finality' — and for this transient kind of finality we need identity, morality and truth.

Glossaries

The theory of histories&discourses, as expounded in this book, makes intensive use of semantic differentiations and distinctions which, in turn, presuppose unities of differences for their realisation. Complementary concepts have played a particular role in this, from suppositions and presuppositions to system and environment. Finally, mechanisms of synthesis for the creation of order, and diverse mechanisms of interruption as instruments of contingency treatment, have been introduced, which may not be widely known in this form.

To make it easier for the readers to survey these conceptual instruments of theory design, they are listed in the following glossary. The resulting assembly of lists demonstrates, at the same time, in the most compact form possible, the basic outline of the theory of histories&discourses as it has been developed in this book.

A. *Unities of differences{/}*
   Contingency {possibility/selection}
   Selection {supposition/presupposition}
   Categories {semantic differentiations/distinction}
   Model of reality {categories/semantic differentiations}
   Culture programme {redundancy/innovation of programme components and programme applications}
   Consciousness {reference/object of reference}
   Agent {cognitive autonomy/social orientation}

Time {before/after} or {here/there}
Space {here/there} or {now/immediately}
Reality {space/time}
Present time {space/time}
Society {model of reality/culture programme}
Reality model&culture programme {histories/
  discourses}
Sense {cognition/communication}
Histories&discourses {action-communications/communica-
  tion-actions}
History {own history/other histories}
Discourse {active/inactive discourse participations}
Speaking {semiotic materiality/meaning}
Identity {self-description/other-description}
Morality {good, inclusion/evil, exclusion}
Good, evil {responsible/irresponsible}
Truth {true/false}

B. *Complementarities*

Model of reality/culture programme
Selection/contingency
Observables/non-observables
Continuity/discontinuity
Consciousness, reference/entities
Supposition/presupposition
Process/structure
Cognition, consciousness/communication
Reality/present time
Space/time
Sense/time
Interaction/communication
Agent/society
Culture/society/agent
Semiotic materiality/meaning
System/environment

C. *Mechanisms of synthesis*

Histories synthesise actions
Actions synthesise events

Discourses synthesise communications
Communications synthesise semiotic materialities

D. Mechanisms of interruption

Time divisions (past, present, future): process interrupters
Reflexivity: continuity interrupter
Schemata, operative fictions: contingency interrupters
Morality: legitimation interrupter
Truth: justification interrupter

Selected References

Assmann, Aleida & Jan Assmann: 'Das Gestern im Heute. Medien und soziales Gedächtnis.' In: K. Merten, S. J. Schmidt & S. Weischenberg (ed.), *Die Wirklichkeit der Medien*. Opladen: Westdeutscher Verlag 1994, 114-140.
Ciompi, Luc: *Die emotionalen Grandlagen des Denkens. Entwurf einer fraktalen Affektlogik*. Göttingen: Vandenhoek & Ruprecht 1997.
Feilke, Helmuth: *Common sense-Kompetenz. Überlegungen zu einer Theorie des 'sympathischen' and 'natürlichen' Meinens and Verstehens*. Frankfurt/M.: Suhrkamp 1994.
Giesecke, Michael: *Von den Mythen der Buchkultur zu den Visionen der Informationsgesellschaft*. Frankfurt/M.: Suhrkamp 2002.
Hall, Stuart (ed): *Representation: Cultural Representations and Signifying Practices: Culture, Media and Identities*. London: Sage 1997.
Hegel, Georg Wilhelm Friedrich: *Wissenschaft der Logik*. Bde. I-III. Leipzig: Fromann 1965.
Jahraus, Oliver: *Theorieschleife. Systemtheorie, Dekonstruktion und Medientheorie*. Wien: Passagen Verlag 2001.
Janich, Peter: 'Verlust der Realität? Ein abendländisches Gedanken-Los?' In: G. Zurstiege (Hg.), *Festschrift für die Wirklichkeit*. Wiesbaden: Westdeutscher Verlag 2000, 13-26.
Janich, Peter: *Was ist Wahrheit? Eine philosophische Einführung*. München: Beck, 5. Auflage. 2000.
Jünger, Sebastian: *Kognition, Kommunikation, Kultur. Aspekte integrativer Theoriearbeit*. Wiesbaden: Deutscher Universitätsverlag 2002.
Kellner, Douglas: *Media Culture. Cultural Studies, Identity and Politics between the Modern and the Postmodern*. London-New York: Routledge 1998.
Krämer, Sybille: *Sprache, Sprechakt, Kommunikation. Sprachtheoretische Positionen des 20. Jahrhunderts*. Frankfurt/M.: Suhrkamp 2001.
Luhmann, Niklas: 'Ethik als Reflexionstheorie der Moral.' In: Ders., *Gesellschaftsstruktur and Semantik. Studien zur Wissenssoziologie der modernen Gesellschaft*, Bd. 3. Frankfurt/M.: Suhrkamp 1989, 358-447.

Luhmann, Niklas: *Paradigm lost: Über die ethische Reflexion der Moral.* Frankfurt/M.: Suhrkamp 1990.
Luhmann, Niklas: *Die Wissenschaft der Gesellschaft.* Frankfurt/M.: Suhrkamp 1990.
Merten, Klaus (1977): *Kommunikation. Eine Begriffs- und Prozessanalyse.* Opladen: Westdeutscher Verlag 1977.
Mitterer, Josef: *Die Flucht aus der Beliebigkeit.* Frankfurt/M: Fischer 2001.
Roth, Gerhard: *Fühlen, Denken, Handeln. Wie das Gehirn unser Verhalten steuert.* Frankfurt/M.: Suhrkamp 2001.
Rusch, Gebhard: 'Verstehen verstehen. Ein Versuch aus konstruktivistischer Sicht.' In: N. Luhmann & K. E. Schorr (Hg.), *Zwischen Intransparenz and Verstehen. Fragen an die Pädagogik.* Frankfurt/M.: Suhrkamp 1986, 40-71.
Rusch, Gebhard: *Erkenntnis, Wissenschaft, Geschichte. Von einem konstruktivistischen Standpunkt.* Frankfurt/M.: Suhrkamp 1987.
Rusch, Gebhard: 'Eine Kommunikationstheorie für kognitive Systeme.' In: G. Rusch & S. J. Schmidt (ed.), *Konstruktivismus in der Medien- and Kommunikationswissenschaft.* Frankfurt/M.: Suhrkamp 1999, 150–184 (DELFIN 1997).
Schapp, Wilhelm: *In Geschichten verstrickt.* Leer: Rautenberg 1953.
Schapp, Wilhelm: *Philosophie der Geschichten.* Leer: Rautenberg 1959.
Schlosser, Gerhard: *Einheit der Welt und Einheitswissenschaft. Grundlegung einer allgemeinen Systemtheorie.* Braunschweig/Wiesbaden: Vieweg 1993 (Wissenschaftstheorie, Wissenschaft und Philosophie Bd. 37)
Schmidt, Siegfried J. & Guido Zurstiege (2000): *Orientierung Kommunikationswissenschaft. Was sie kann, was sie will.* Reinbek bei Hamburg: Rowohlt 2000.
Schmidt, Siegfried J.: *Texttheorie. Probleme einer Linguistik der sprachlichen Kommunikation.* München: Fink 1973.
Schmidt, Siegfried J.: *Die Selbstorganisation des Sozialsystems Literatur im 18. Jahrhundert.* Frankfurt/M.: Suhrkamp 1989.
Schmidt, Siegfried J.: *Kognitive Autonomie und soziale Orientierung: Konstruktivistische Bemerkungen zum Zusammenhang von Kognition, Kommunikation, Medien and Kultur.* Frankfurt/M.: Suhrkamp 1994.
Schmidt, Siegfried J.: *Die Zähmung des Blicks. Konstruktivismus – Empirie – Wissenschaft.* Frankfurt/M.: Suhrkamp 1998.
Schmidt, Siegfried J.: *Kalte Faszination. Medien Kultur Wissenschaft in der Mediengesellschaft.* Weilerswist: Velbrück Wissenschaft 2000.
Schmidt, Siegfried J.: *Unternehmenskultur. Die Grundlage für den wirtschaftlichen Erfolg von Unternehmen.* Weilerswist: Velbrück Wissenschaft 2004.

von Foerster, Heinz: *Wissen und Gewissen. Versuch einer Brücke. Herausgegeben von Siegfried J. Schmidt.* Frankfurt/M.: Suhrkamp 1993.
von Glasersfeld, Ernst: *Radikaler Konstruktivismus. Ideen, Ergebnisse, Probleme.* Frankfurt/M.: Suhrkamp 1996. (*Radical Constructivism: A Way of Knowing and Learning.* London: The Falmer Press 1995. Transl. by W. K. Köck).
von Weizsäcker, Carl Friedrich: *Der Garten des Menschlichen. Beiträge zur geschichtlichen Anthropologie.* München: Hanser 1980.